Uncommon Worship

25 Innovative Services

Nick Fawcett

kevin
mayhew

Dedicated with grateful thanks to
John and Rose Elliston and family,
remembering kindness shown, friendship shared,
encouragement offered and inspiration given.

First published in 2004 by
KEVIN MAYHEW LTD
Buxhall, Stowmarket, Suffolk IP14 3BW
Email: info@kevinmayhewltd.com

9 8 7 6 5 4 3 2 1 0

ISBN 1 84417 295 3
Catalogue Number 1500723

Cover design by Angela Selfe
Edited by Katherine Laidler
Typesetting by Kevin Whomes

Printed and bound in Great Britain

CONTENTS

INTRODUCTION

There's no getting away from it: church services can be dull if not downright boring. That's not intended as a criticism of those who lead worship; it's more to question the nature of worship itself and to ask whether the patterns we adopt communicate as effectively as we might like to imagine. That goes for each and every tradition, because, make no mistake, we can all get stuck in a rut, whether we follow a formal liturgy, a 'hymn sandwich', or an ostensibly spontaneous form of worship. All of these work for some people, some of the time, though probably even the most ardent of churchgoers find their thoughts wandering in a typical Sunday service more often than they'd care to admit. If that's true of committed Christians, how much more must it be so for those on the fringes or the occasional visitor? The language and concepts we Christians use tend to be far removed from people's daily experience, yet language is typically the be all and end all in worship, our other senses rarely being engaged.

In this book, through 25 themed services – each of which explores facets of our humanity and how these relate to God – I have attempted to offer innovative ideas that might help address this problem. There are services focusing on sight, sound, scent, taste and touch; others celebrate music, humour, poetry and drama; others again explore creative talents ranging from needlework to handicraft, flower-arranging to dance; and others still make use of puzzles and quiz questions. The services can be used in a variety of contexts, flexibility being needed according to the 'audience' you have in mind. You may wish simply to breathe variety into your usual Sunday fare, opening up new horizons to your regular worshippers. If so, you could stage a series of 'uncommon worship' services over successive weeks, using, say, the five services devoted to sight or to sound, or the four under 'Using our gifts', 'Using our imagination' or 'Using our minds'. On the other hand, there is much here for those planning family services, many of the themes readily lending themselves to all-age worship. Alternatively, your concern might be to reach beyond your usual congregation to the 'unchurched', in which case you could hold Guest Services each month, finding sufficient resources in this book to cover two years. If you opt for the latter, make sure that you publicise the services as thoroughly as possible, emphasising their innovative nature. Also encourage members of the congregation to invite friends, family members, neighbours and colleagues – the importance of the personal touch cannot be overemphasised.

I have attempted to supply all the ingredients needed for the services I've outlined, and where that has not been possible I offer guidelines as to where resources can be found. The service plans include suggestions for visual/audio resources, hymns, Bible readings and prayers, together with outline orders of service (the hymns can be found in *Anglican Hymns Old and New, Methodist Hymns* and *The Source*, all published by Kevin Mayhew). I have also included a short Introduction to each service, and, bar a few exceptions, what I have termed a Talk précis. Note that I have purposely avoided the word 'sermon' – each service is designed as far as possible to speak for itself, so any talk given should be kept short, no more than five minutes at most. The service order at the end of each section shows how the material can be fitted into a relatively traditional framework if desired, but don't shy away from being more adventurous, particularly if you are looking to reach out to those beyond the Church. You might wish to dispense with a talk altogether or merge it with the Introduction; you might prefer to use a series of relevant Bible verses instead of long Bible readings; you might make much more use of silence or music, or you might want to sing several hymns and songs together rather than at regular intervals during the service. Remember, though, that you are not looking to be different as some sort of gimmick but solely to enrich people's worship through opening up new dimensions and possibilities.

A few words of warning and practical advice are in order.

- First, in those services concerned with the senses, be alert to those with disabilities – the partially sighted and aurally impaired, the physically disabled and so forth – those, in other words, who will struggle to participate in the service as fully as others and who indeed might be hurt or angered by an insensitive handling of the theme.

- Second, if you plan to use recorded music or visual props, including computer PowerPoint presentations, ensure everything is prepared carefully and safely well in advance, and double-check before the service that all is in order (if possible, ensure there are back-up facilities should a bulb/computer/hi-fi system fail). While you are not looking for perfection, you still want things to run as smoothly and professionally as possible.

- Third, where music or poetry are incorporated, ensure a good balance between old and new, light and heavy, to ensure that as far as possible all tastes are catered for.

- Fourth, when handling foodstuffs, take steps to guarantee hygiene at all times.

- Fifth, where puzzles and quizzes are used – and indeed any visual aids – ensure that these are clearly visible to all in the congregation.

- Sixth, where possible involve the congregation in the collecting and creating of visual aids so that they feel a sense of ownership in the service.

- Seventh, obtain copyright permission if needed for any of the resources you use, assuming that these are not already covered by a copyright licence.
- Eighth, explain carefully what is happening in parts of the service that might otherwise cause confusion; strangers to the church might otherwise be left feeling awkward and uncomfortable.

I have used many of the ideas in this book myself during the course of my ministry, each time receiving very positive feedback. Of course, not every suggestion may work for you, and it is important that you tailor the resources provided to your own requirements, putting your own stamp on the service in question so that it carries the all-important ring of sincerity. It is my sincere hope that you will find something in these pages to help you explore new avenues of worship and in turn open up new horizons to those within and outside the Church.

NICK FAWCETT

Section One
USING OUR SENSES

SIGHT

1 It's a wonderful world

A celebration of creation through slides, words and music

The aim of this service is to focus on and celebrate the beauty of the natural world in all its rich variety. The emphasis is on celebrating all that is good in the world, everything that causes us to catch our breath in wonder, rejoice and give thanks.

Key verses

When I look at the universe, the work of your hands, the moon and stars you have brought into being, what is humankind that you are concerned about us; how is it you care about mere mortals?
Psalm 8:3-4

Resources

- As a key resource, I recommend using photographic slides and music, or, if you have access to the necessary resources, a series of PowerPoint presentations depicting some or all of the following:
  a. For first sequence: pictures of Earth photographed from space (details of slides and downloadable photographs can be found on the NASA website) and/or sunsets, clouds, the moon, night sky, cloud formations, etc.
  b. For second sequence: pictures of seascapes, rivers, streams, lakes, waterfalls, etc.
  c. For third sequence: waste disposal landfill site, local tip, fly tipping, littered streets, recycling depot.
  d. For fourth sequence: pictures of mountain peaks, birds and animals, pastoral scenes, flowers and gardens, woodland, snow scene, etc.
- Pictures/posters of country scenes, etc., displayed around the church.
- Floral displays.
- Slide projector or backlight projector, and screen.
- Hi-fi and amplification system (more hi-tech resources will be needed if you plan to show pictures in the form of a PowerPoint presentation).
- Recorded music (see *Suggested music* below).

Suggested music

- *It's a wonderful world* sung by Louis Armstrong
- 'The heavens are telling' from *The Creation* (Haydn)
- 'Shepherd's Song' from *Pastoral Symphony* (No. 6) (Beethoven)
- 'Mars' from *The Planets* (Holst)
- First movement from *Moonlight Sonata* (Beethoven)
- *Water Music* (Handel)
- *Finlandia* (Sibelius)

- Atmospheric music – for example, Celtic music; panpipes; *Oxygene* (Jean Michel Jarre); *To the Unknown Man* (Vangelis).

Suggested hymns

- I lift my eyes to the quiet hills
- O Lord, my God (How great thou art)
- Morning has broken
- O worship the King
- Jesus is Lord! Creation's voice proclaims it   260
- Praise to the Lord, the Almighty, the King of creation
- Lord, you created a world full of splendour
- Give to our God immortal praise
- Lord of beauty, thine the splendour
- All creatures of our God and King
- Every bird, every tree
- For the fruits of his creation   342
- When morning gilds the skies   276
- Let all the world in every corner sing
- All things praise thee, Lord most high
- For the beauty of meadows, for the grandeur of trees

Introduction

We are here today to celebrate the wonder of creation in all its loveliness. Through words of the Psalms and Jesus, through hymns and songs of praise, through music inspired by creation and through scenes of the world and the cosmos, we will reflect on the beauty that surrounds us and offer our response in worship.

Suggested readings

For readings see *Order of Service*.

Talk précis

Can we prove the existence of God from the natural world? No. Is everything in nature beautiful? No. Does contemplating the created order automatically lead us to worship and celebration? Again, the answer has to be no. Much in the world is ugly, even repulsive; natural disasters are frequent, disease is a daily threat, and for many creatures the struggle for life is harsh, bloody and brutal, and only the strongest survive. Though many aspects of the world around us may indeed support faith, many others count against it, or at least remind us that creation awaits its final fulfilment. Yet if all this is so, it is nonetheless true that countless people across the years have drawn inspiration from nature, finding there much that speaks of God's love and purpose, and that gives us cause for celebration and thanksgiving. Look at the night sky, they say, or at a sunset; at the beauty of a flower or the wonder of the human body; at the vastness of the ocean or the grandeur of mountains: does this not suggest some creative purpose? The answer, of course, as with so much, is that it depends how you look at it. To the sceptic the answer will be 'No', but to the eye of faith it will be a resounding 'Yes!'

We are reminded today not only of the wonder of creation and all it says to us, but also of how much we have to give thanks for and celebrate, each of which we can so easily forget to do. Alongside these, however, is a call to live as faithful stewards, doing our best to use wisely what God has given, thinking not just of ourselves but of others. As we worship God, then, let us also consider our lifestyles and commit ourselves afresh to showing our gratitude through responsible living and faithful discipleship.

Prayers

Praise

Creator God,
    ruler of space and time –
    before all,
    within all,
    beyond all –
    in awe and wonder
    we come to worship.

We can never fully fathom the vastness of space
    or the complexities of our universe,
    but, despite all that baffles and confuses,
    we glimpse your power,
    your purpose,
    your presence.
So, then,
    in awe and wonder
    we come to worship.

We are part of an imperfect world,
    scarred by sorrow and suffering,
    death and disease,
    conflict and cruelty,
    yet there is also so much good and loveliness within it,
    so much that causes us to catch our breath in delight
    and respond in celebration.
So, then,
    in awe and wonder
    we come to worship.

Sovereign God,
    Lord of all,
    giver of all,
    open our eyes to the richness of creation
    and to everything you would say to us through it.
Amen.

Intercession

Gracious God,
    we pray today for those who cannot see
    or whose sight is severely impaired.
Let the light of your love shine within them,
    to equip, encourage and enable.

We pray for those denied sight from birth
    and those who have lost this faculty through illness,
        accident or injury:
    all who must live in a world of semi or total darkness,
    dependent on their other senses
    to interact with and interpret their immediate environment.
Let the light of your love shine within them,
    to equip, encourage and enable.

We pray for all whose sight is declining:
    those living with the prospect of accelerating impairment,
    any joy felt at things seen tinged by the knowledge
    that, one day, they might see them no longer.
Let the light of your love shine within them,
    to equip, encourage and enable.

We pray for those who work to save or restore sight:
    scientists, surgeons, opticians and ophthalmologists,
    charities, societies and research departments,
    guide-dog associations and trainers,
    individual carers and support groups.
Let the light of your love shine within them,
    to equip, encourage and enable.

Gracious God,
    may eyes be opened,
    sight restored,
    vision renewed,
    and, where this is not possible,
    bring support and strength for each day.
In the name of Christ we ask it.
Amen.

Confession

Living God,
    we are reminded today that, if only we would look,
    there is so much around us to enthral,
    enchant,

enthuse
and excite us –
so much beauty and variety to stir the heart
and capture the imagination.
For closing our eyes to the wonder of the world,
   forgive us.

We have grown over-familiar,
   taking for granted what once held our attention,
   inured to the special in the ordinary.
For closing our eyes to the wonder of the world,
   forgive us.

We have been turned in on ourselves,
   wrapped up in our concerns and problems,
   so focused on them that we have seen little else.
For closing our eyes to the wonder of the world,
   forgive us.

We have been too busy to stop and stare,
   rushing frenetically from one thing to another
   and consequently losing sight of life's simple treasures.
For closing our eyes to the wonder of the world,
   forgive us.

We have abused your creation,
   despoiling,
   plundering,
   wasting
   and abusing.
Instead of seeing it as a gift
   we have seen it as a right;
   instead of acting as faithful stewards
   we have acted carelessly and thoughtlessly,
   repeatedly frittering away the riches you have entrusted to us.
For closing our eyes to the wonder of the world,
   forgive us.

Living God,
   open our eyes afresh to the loveliness of creation,
   the awesomeness of the universe,
   the abundance of this Earth;
   the beauty that is everywhere surrounds us.
Rekindle in us a sense of childlike wonder.
Restore the ability to pause and ponder.
Remind us each day of all we have to celebrate.
For closing our eyes to the wonder of the world,
   forgive us.

In Christ's name we pray.
Amen.

Thanksgiving
Loving God,
    we want to thank you for this world you have given us:
    so full of delight,
    so endowed with beauty.

For all that captivates and inspires,
    moving us to wonder,
    joy,
    amazement,
    Lord of all,
    receive our thanks.

For all that fascinates and intrigues,
    moving us to ponder,
    enquire,
    investigate,
    Lord of all,
    receive our thanks.

For all that soothes and calms,
    filling us with tranquillity,
    contentment,
    inner peace,
    Lord of all,
    receive our thanks.

For all that encourages and intrigues,
    giving us hope,
    meaning,
    a sense of being part of your eternal purpose,
    Lord of all,
    receive our thanks.

Loving God,
    for this world,
    this life,
    this day you have given us;
    for eyes to see
    and minds to take it all in,
    we give you our grateful worship.
Lord of all,
    receive our thanks.
Amen.

Closing prayers
Go out into the world rejoicing,
    for God is waiting to meet you and surprise you
    with the beauty of his presence.
In the song of a blackbird,
    the hooting of an owl,
    the cry of a fox;
    in the opening of a bud,
    the fragrance of a flower,
    the falling of a leaf;
    in the murmur of the breeze,
    the rushing of the wind,
    the howling of the gale;
    in the babbling of the brook,
    the rippling of the stream,
    the crashing of the waves;
    in the peace of the meadows,
    the freedom of the hills,
    the grandeur of the mountains;
    in the cry of a baby,
    the laughter of children,
    the hum of conversation;
    in the pat on a shoulder,
    the handshake of welcome,
    the embrace of a loved one;
    in the noise of the factory,
    the routine of the office,
    the bustle of the shop –
    God is here,
    God is there,
    God is everywhere.
Go then,
    and walk with him,
    in the light of his love,
    and the fullness of life.
Amen.

Faithful God,
    we go with gratitude to celebrate the beauty of your world,
    the beauty of life,
    the beauty of all you have given.
To you belong praise and worship,
    now and always.
Amen.

Order of Service

Bible passages and prayers are to be read as a voiceover while visuals are screened and music played; the congregation, therefore, need to pray with their eyes open. The music indicated below is just a suggestion; you may have other ideas.

- Key verses
- Introduction
- Hymn
- First visual sequence: Pictures of Earth photographed from space and/or sunsets, clouds, the moon, during which read **Psalm 19:1-6; 104:1-4; 147:8**, accompanied by 'Mars' from *The Planets* (Holst) or the slow movement of the *Moonlight Sonata* (Beethoven)
- Prayer of praise
- Hymn
- Second visual sequence: Pictures of the sea, rivers, streams, lakes, during which read Psalm **65:7; 95:5; 29:3** (for sea); **Psalm 65:9-10** (for streams/rivers) accompanied by Handel's *Water Music*
- Prayer of intercession
- Third visual sequence: Pictures of waste disposal landfill site, local tip, fly tipping, littered streets, recycling depot (no music)
- Prayer of confession (read after sequence, not as voiceover)
- Hymn
- Fourth visual sequence: Pictures of flowers, trees, birds, animals, mountains, pastoral scenes, woodland, snow scene, during which read **Matthew 6:28-30** (flowers); **Matthew 6:26-27** (birds); **Psalm 50:10-11; 147:9** (animals); **Psalm 90:2; 95:3-4** (mountains); **Psalm 147:15-18** (snow and ice); **Psalm 65:11-13; 145:4-5** (general); accompanied by *It's a wonderful world* (Louis Armstrong)
- Prayer of thanksgiving
- Hymn
- Closing prayers

2   Look at it this way

A fun family service making use of unusual pictures

The aim of this service is to emphasise that God repeatedly chooses to work in unexpected ways, opening up new dimensions into the apparent realities of a situation.

Key verses

We proclaim Christ crucified, an offensive idea to the Jews and plain folly to others, but to those whom God has called, whether Jews or Greeks, this message of Christ is both the power and wisdom of God. *1 Corinthians 1:23-24*

Resources

For this service you will need pictures of items/situations in which things are not quite as they seem. You could either draw/photograph your own, make use of suitably gifted people in your congregation, or browse through puzzle books in your local bookshop/library. The following are just some of the visual aids you could make use of:

- Enlarged photographs or drawings of familiar objects viewed from unusual angles.
- Pictures that appear to illustrate one situation but that, in fact, once more of the picture is revealed, depict quite another.
- Pictures of illusions (see Appendix, page 237).

Suggested hymns

- Open our eyes, Lord
- Turn your eyes upon Jesus
- Mine eyes have seen the glory
- Sometimes a light surprises
- Lord, the light of your love is shining
- Look what God has done (And his love goes on and on)

Introduction

Appearances, we sometimes say, can be deceptive. Our first impression of people may turn out to be wide of the mark; their true colours, once we get to know them, can be very different than we imagined. An offer that looks too good to miss can, once we've had time to survey the small print, prove to be a scam. A banknote or painting may be a forgery, a video or computer game a pirate copy, and a seemingly immaculate second-hand car a recycled write-off. Things are by no means always what they seem. Not that this is always a bad thing. Sometimes a glimpse of hidden depths, unexplored possibilities, new dimensions leaves us pleasantly surprised, realising that there is far more to a person or situation than we had previously imagined. For a life lived in faith that is always so, for God is constantly able to surprise us with his love, turning situations upside down and inside out.

Today, through various unusual images, we recognise how there can be more to things than meets the eye, and we apply that to faith, reminding ourselves that God is always able to do more than we either ask or expect.

Suggested readings

- Isaiah 53:1-12
- 1 Corinthians 1:18-25
- Ephesians 3:20-21

Talk précis

The film *The Passion of the Christ* controversially highlighted for many the awfulness of crucifixion and the agony that Jesus must have experienced on the cross. Imagine that you had been standing there as he died, hearing his groans, seeing the blood drip from his hands and feet, watching the life ebb slowly from his broken body – what would you have made of it all? Would you have seen this as the triumph of God's love, a display of his power, the vindication of his purpose? I doubt it. More likely, especially if you had followed Jesus during his lifetime, it would have come across as an unmitigated tragedy, the end of your hopes, and further evidence, as if any were needed, of the cruelty to which humankind can stoop. Yet, as Paul reminds the Corinthians, 'we proclaim Christ crucified, an offensive idea to the Jews and plain folly to others, but to those whom God has called, whether Jews or Greeks, this message of Christ is both the power and wisdom of God' (1 Corinthians 1:23-24). Those words illustrate how our interpretation of what we see can differ, and if that's true of life in general it's true for the Christian in a more important way, for it reminds us that our perception of the world is very different to God's. We may look at a situation and consider it hopeless. We may look at a person and believe them beyond redemption. We may look at a problem and feel there's nothing more we can do to solve it. We may look at our resources and feel they're inadequate to meet a task. Yet in each case there is more than meets the eye, for God's love offers a new perspective on life, his power bringing a different dimension, his grace opening up ever-new possibilities. So often, with God, things are other than they first seem. Remember, then, next time things look bleak, next time you're not sure where to turn, next time you're tempted to give up on a situation; remember that where *you* see obstacles God can see opportunities, where *you* see weakness he sees strength, and where all seems dark he so often is bringing light.

Prayers

Praise
Living God,
    we worship you again today
    for your life-changing, world-shaping, earth-shattering power,
    through which you continue to work so wonderfully,

despite everything that seems to undermine and deny
your loving purpose.
For taking what is,
    and creating what shall be,
    Lord of all, we praise you.

We marvel at your hand in creation:
    sustaining the universe,
    bringing order out of chaos,
    imparting the gift of life –
    day by day your love working to bring all things
    to fulfilment in Christ.
For taking what is,
    and creating what shall be,
    Lord of all, we praise you.

We marvel at your hand in human lives:
    the way you call before we even know you,
    and continue to prompt,
    teach,
    guide
    and forgive,
    offering new beginnings however often we might fail you.
For taking what is,
    and creating what shall be,
    Lord of all, we praise you.

We marvel at your hand in daily experience:
    the experiences we have had time and again of your transforming
        grace,
    using us in ways that defy our expectations,
    overcoming obstacles that appeared insurmountable,
    turning apparent cul-de-sacs into avenues of opportunity,
    and bringing light out of darkness,
    laughter out of tears,
    peace out of turmoil,
    and hope out of despair.
For taking what is,
    and creating what shall be,
    Lord of all, we praise you.

We marvel at your hand in the world:
    the way, despite so much pain and evil,
    so much that thwarts your loving purpose,
    you are still able to stir our hearts,
    quicken our consciences,
    pursue justice
    and inspire change.

For taking what is,
  and creating what shall be,
  Lord of all, we praise you.

Living God,
  for all you have done,
  all you are doing,
  all you *can* do
  and all you *will* do,
  receive our grateful worship,
  in the name of Christ.
Amen.

Thanksgiving
Almighty God,
  we thank you for the message of Christ crucified and risen,
  and for everything that tells us about life touched by your hand.

Where darkness seemed total,
  light broke through.
Lord,
  we thank you.

Where evil seemed victorious,
  good triumphed.
Lord,
  we thank you.

Where hatred seemed in charge,
  love conquered.
Lord,
  we thank you.

Where sorrow seemed intractable,
  joy swept it away.
Lord,
  we thank you.

Where death seemed final,
  life burst from the tomb.
Lord,
  we thank you.

Where despair seemed to spell the end,
  hope sprang eternal.
Lord,
  we thank you.

For your loving power
   and gracious purpose
   that goes on surprising us,
   revealing possibilities we never dreamt of
   and truths we never imagined.
Lord,
   we thank you.
Amen.

Confession

Loving God
   though we speak of all you can do in our lives,
   so often we fail to see it when it matters.
Instead of using the resources you put at our disposal
   we struggle along in our own strength,
   looking to muddle along as best we can,
   forgetting the strength, guidance, love and mercy
   you so long to show us
For glimpsing so much
   but seeing so little,
   forgive us, O Lord.

Even when we do see, we do not always accept,
   preferring sometimes to shut our eyes and close our minds,
   for as well as promise your love brings challenge:
   a call to recognise our faults,
   acknowledge our misplaced priorities,
   and, where necessary, to change.
For glimpsing so much
   but seeing so little,
   forgive us, O Lord.

It's the same, Lord, with others,
   our eyes too often being closed to their potential –
   the way you use them to fulfil your purpose
   and speak through them to challenge, teach or guide.
Instead of seeing the true person beneath the surface,
   we see only a caricature shaped by our own perception,
   what seems to be, rather than what is and what might become.
For glimpsing so much
   but seeing so little,
   forgive us, O Lord.

Once more, even when we do see,
   we do not always wish to look,
   for we find it hard to revise our opinions,
   to accept we've been wrong about people,

to realise that we have as much to receive as to give
and that others have gifts, qualities and insights that we don't.
For glimpsing so much
　　but seeing so little,
　　forgive us, O Lord.

Loving God,
　　in so many ways we lose sight of your ability to change the world,
　　transform society,
　　renew your Church,
　　overturn situations
　　and shape lives,
　　the narrowness of our vision so often shutting out
　　and obstructing your will.
For glimpsing so much
　　but seeing so little,
　　forgive us, O Lord.

Help us to see with your eyes,
　　and to be open to all you can do within us
　　and within all,
　　through Jesus Christ our Lord.
Amen.

Intercession
Lord God,
　　we find it hard sometimes to believe our world can change,
　　for there are so many things that,
　　despite the prayers of your people across the years,
　　remain frustratingly and depressingly the same.

We think of poverty,
　　as real today as it has ever been,
　　millions struggling even to survive,
　　denied proper food,
　　housing,
　　water,
　　education,
　　medical care
　　and so much else.
Though we pray for justice, respect and opportunity for all,
　　their plight continues,
　　inequalities between rich and poor
　　growing ever more pronounced.
Lord of all,
　　restore faith,
　　rekindle vision,
　　and grant new beginnings in our broken world.

We think of lands torn by war,
　　countries racked by suffering and sorrow,
　　hatred and slaughter,
　　hostility fuelled by tribal, ethnic, ideological or religious divisions.
Especially we think of the Middle East,
　　so deeply divided,
　　so cruelly scarred by fear,
　　suspicion,
　　hatred
　　and indiscriminate bloodshed.
Though we pray for peace, dialogue and a just settlement,
　　it is hard to believe that a solution will ever be found.
Lord of all,
　　restore faith,
　　rekindle vision,
　　and grant new beginnings in our broken world.

We think of our own society
　　and the evils that seem to have become endemic to it:
　　alcohol and drug abuse,
　　violence and vandalism,
　　pornography and paedophilia,
　　crime and corruption.
Though we pray for change,
　　there seems little reason for confidence,
　　the problems seeming to grow worse instead of better.
Lord of all,
　　restore faith,
　　rekindle vision,
　　and grant new beginnings in our broken world.

We pray for the Church,
　　struggling to maintain a witness in an increasingly secular society,
　　yet so many traditions, in this country at least,
　　struggling to survive, let alone to change the world.
Though we pray for renewal,
　　the statistics year by year paint a different picture,
　　and hope is sometimes stretched to the limit.
Lord of all,
　　restore faith,
　　rekindle vision,
　　and grant new beginnings in our broken world.

Lord,
　　remind us that, though we may not see it,
　　you are always at work,
　　and that, despite all that conspires against you,
　　your purpose will finally prevail.

Teach us that our understanding is partial
   and our picture incomplete,
   and so, however things may seem,
   help us still to trust,
   still to pray
   and still to work for your kingdom.
Lord of all,
   restore faith,
   rekindle vision,
   and grant new beginnings in our broken world.
Amen.

Closing prayer
God of surprises,
   go with us now
   and open our hearts to meet you in every aspect of life,
   even when we might least expect it
   and where we might least think to look,
   through Jesus Christ our Lord.
Amen.

Order of Service

- Key verses
- Introduction
- Hymn
- Prayer of praise
- Display of pictures
- Reading
- Display of pictures
- Prayer of thanksgiving
- Hymn
- Display of pictures
- Talk
- Prayer of confession
- Hymn
- Prayer of intercession
- Hymn
- Closing prayer

3 Every picture tells a story

A service of intercession using pictures, words and music

The aim of this service is to bring a visual element to intercession and to show how such prayers can and should be a part of daily life.

Key verse

Pray without ceasing . . .
1 Thessalonians 5:17

Resources

- Take slides or digital photographs of local places and institutions (some, of course, will only be found in large towns and cities, but many will be found locally or nearby): for example, shops, schools, factories, offices, suburban street, hospital, health centres, police station, fire station, Social Security offices, employment centre, cemetery, town hall, nursing home, mother-and-toddler club, park, pubs, sports centre, rubbish tip, bank, charity shop, garden centre, prison.
- Borrow or hire (from a denominational/national/international charity) slides or photographs illustrating situations of worldwide concern: for example, poverty, hunger, AIDS.
- Photograph/scan in headlines from national newspapers relating to current issues in the news.
- Display cuttings from national and local papers, together with further local photographs, around the walls of the church, each supplemented by enlarged headlines/titles.

Suggested music

- *Give peace a chance* (John Lennon)
- *Imagine* (John Lennon)
- *I'd like to teach the world to sing* (The New Seekers)
- *Ebony and ivory* (Paul McCartney)
- *Streets of London* (Ralph McTell)
- *Feed the world* (Band Aid; suitable if the service takes place around Christmas)

Suggested hymns

- When the Church of Jesus
- Beauty for brokenness (God of the poor)
- For the healing of the nations
- Where cross the crowded ways of life
- Jesu, Jesu
- Brother, sister, let me serve you
- Put peace into each other's hands
- Heal our nation
- Lord, you have given yourself for our healing

Introduction

How should we pray for others? What should we pray for? Where should we start and where finish? All these and countless other questions spring to mind when it comes to prayers of intercession. We want to pray, to express our concern and to show our love, in some way to make a difference, but we're not sure sometimes where to start or how to go about it. In this service we approach such prayer using our eyes as well as our minds, pictures as well as words, exploring how all of life can be a prayer, every person, place and moment consecrated simply but sincerely into the hands of God.

Suggested readings

- Matthew 25:31-46
- 1 Thessalonians 5:12-25

Talk précis

'Pray without ceasing', says Paul in his first letter to the Thessalonians. It's a daunting prospect, isn't it, one that suggests some kind of monastic devotion to prayer, and few of us feel called to such a life. Yet when it comes to intercession alone, to praying for others as most of us feel we should, then it's hard sometimes to see how, if we are to pray seriously, we can do anything but pray without ceasing. After all, there are so many people to pray for, so many situations of need, so many known to us, let alone those unknown. If we were to remember each one by name and think meaningfully of them, then probably the list would never be exhausted. Clearly, for most of us such prayer is impossible, and I doubt any of us would for a moment ever attempt it, but where then does that leave our intercessions? All too easily it creates a sense of guilt, a feeling that we aren't doing enough, even that we're letting people down. Yet does this perhaps indicate that we've become too hung up on words in prayer, imagining that unless we articulate our thoughts in a certain way and prescribed attitude God will fail to hear us? Paul's words concerning unceasing prayer surely suggest that prayer is far wider than we might imagine, more to do with living with a constant sense of God's presence and consecrating every moment to him. In terms of intercession that means lifting each situation we find ourselves in and each person we meet simply and sincerely into God's presence, asking his blessing upon them and asking also what response he might be asking for from us. Whether at home or work, in the supermarket or sports centre, in church or at the football match, at the health centre or the benefit office – in other words, in all life's varied situations – we are rubbing shoulders with those whom God infinitely values. Through recognising that truth and responding to it, not only our prayer life but life in general will be enriched beyond measure.

Prayers

Praise and thanksgiving
Sovereign God,
    we rejoice that you are not distant,
    removed from our daily experience

and unconcerned about the situations we face,
   but present among us,
   intimately involved in the routine business of our lives,
   sharing our joys and sorrows,
   hopes and fears,
   successes and disappointments,
   pleasure and pain.
For the knowledge that we matter to you,
   and that all things are in your hands,
   receive our praise.

We thank you that you care about our needs,
   and are always looking to respond –
   eager to support,
   strengthen,
   comfort
   and encourage;
   to touch each moment with your grace.
For the knowledge that we matter to you,
   and that all things are in your hands,
   receive our praise.

We rejoice that no person is beyond your love,
   no situation beyond redemption
   and no place beyond your concern.
Wherever we may be, you are there with us,
   longing to lead,
   to bless
   and to nurture.
For the knowledge that we matter to you,
   and that all things are in your hands,
   receive our praise.

Help us as we worship,
   to recognise you are with us now
   and with us always,
   and so may we consecrate life in every part
   into your keeping,
   through Jesus Christ our Lord.
Amen.

Confession
Gracious God,
   though we speak of your daily presence,
   all too often we forget you are near.
We live each day with no thought of your love,
   no reference to your will,

no sense of your purpose
and no recourse to your word.
For the limits we place upon you,
God of all, forgive us.

We worship you on Sunday
and then forget you on Monday,
faith confined to a few moments set aside from the world,
rather than spilling over into our daily routine.
For the limits we place upon you,
God of all, forgive us.

We give you a slot in our lives marked 'religious',
yet so often fail to integrate that with the way we speak and act,
commitment either overlooked
or put aside at our convenience.
For the limits we place upon you,
God of all, forgive us.

We talk about spiritual and secular,
sacred and worldly,
as though these are two spheres set apart,
the one having nothing to do with the other,
whereas you want faith and life to be woven inextricably together.
For the limits we place upon you,
God of all, forgive us.

Through forgetfulness,
laziness,
wilfulness
or faithlessness
we have betrayed our calling
and denied your loving purpose for all.
Speak afresh, through your word,
open our lives in every part to the breath of your Spirit,
and help us to recognise your presence in every place
at every moment.
For the limits we place upon you,
God of all, forgive us.
Amen.

Intercessions

Intercessions for this service are divided into two slots, one focusing
on the local community in which the church is situated, and the
other focusing on world affairs. The prayers are essentially visual,
members of the congregation invited to reflect on the scenes shown
and then to consecrate them to God. Each picture (see *Resources*

above) should be shown for around 15 seconds, the following sentence and response being used after each has been displayed for about half that time:

We bring you our world, Lord.
**Reach out in love,
    and help us to serve.**

Music could be used as backing to the slides (see *Suggested Music* above), this being faded each time the sentence and response is used.

Closing prayer
Walk with us, Lord,
    and teach us to glimpse your presence
    and sense your call
    in every place
    and every person.
Amen.

**Order of
Service**

- Key verses
- Introduction
- Hymn
- Prayer of praise and thanksgiving
- Reading
- Visual intercessions: (1) Our community
- Hymn
- Talk
- Prayer of confession
- Hymn
- Reading
- Visual intercessions: (2) Our world
- Hymn
- Closing prayer

4 Look more closely

A service highlighting the fact that God is present, even though we may not always see him

The aim of this service is to bring home the fact that we can often overlook the ways God is at work in our lives and the world around us, simply because we are too busy to look or because we've become too familiar, no longer seeing what's there before us.

Key verse

The hearing ear and the seeing eye, God has made them both.
Proverbs 20:12

Do you have eyes and fail to see . . . ?
Mark 8:18a

Resources

- For this talk you will need to prepare three quizzes of around fifteen questions each concerning fixtures, fittings and other items within your church building. You might ask, for example, about people's names on commemorative plaques, illustrations on stained glass windows, the publisher of your hymn books/Bibles, the number of people in the congregation, the patterns on prayer mats/pew covers, the number of light bulbs/door handles/chairs, etc.
- Use the poem 'Leisure' by W. H. Davies (see below) to highlight the importance of making time to take in the sights and sounds all around us.
- Prior to the service, arrange for people to bring forward the following items after the talk: bread and wine; a small cross; a lighted candle; a bunch of flowers; an open Bible; a church magazine; a globe (of the world).

Leisure
What is this life if, full of care,
We have no time to stand and stare? –

No time to stand beneath the boughs,
And stare as long as sheep and cows:

No time to see, when woods we pass,
Where squirrels hide their nuts in grass:

No time to see, in broad daylight,
Streams full of stars, like skies at night:

No time to turn at Beauty's glance,
And watch her feet, how they can dance:

No time to wait till her mouth can
Enrich that smile her eyes began?

A poor life this if, full of care,
We have no time to stand and stare.
W. H. Davies (1871-1940)
Reproduced by kind permission of the trustees for W. H. Davies

Suggested hymns

- Teach me, my God and King
- Open our eyes, Lord
- Lord, I was blind, I could not see
- May I never lose sight of you
- I lift my eyes to the quiet hills
- Mine eyes have seen the glory
- Sometimes a light surprises
- All things praise thee, Lord most high
- Lord, you created a world full of splendour

Introduction

When did you last see God at work? What does such language actually mean? And why is it that so many people – the great majority – live each day with no thought or sense of his presence? Those are the sort of questions we're here to consider today, so that through them we might glimpse a little more clearly the way God is actively involved both in *our* lives and the life of the world.

Suggested readings

- Psalm 119:18
- Psalm 26:1-3
- Matthew 6:25-33

Talk précis

How long does it take for something to become familiar? The answer, of course, is not long at all. Hang a new picture in a room and the first few times you go in there it will catch your eye immediately, but before long you will barely even notice it's there. The same holds true in much else, things that once moved us to tears of wonder and joy all too swiftly being taken for granted, even leaving us cold. We may wish it were otherwise, but sadly the old saying 'Familiarity breeds contempt' is repeatedly proven true. Equally, there are times when we cannot see for looking; we are so intent on spotting one thing that we are closed to all kinds of others. Again, we can fail to see occasionally simply because we're less observant than we might imagine. It has been shown by scientists that both our eyes and minds are generally focused on specific objects, which means that much of what we see – indeed, most – is relegated to the periphery, scarcely noted at all. That's precisely what we've seen today in relation to our church building. We gather here week in, week out, so you'd have thought we'd know what there is to see like the back of our hands, but though a few may indeed do just that the rest of us probably rarely notice a host of details here and there. Our eyes are open but we fail to see.

Is that what Jesus meant by his words (Mark 8:18a): 'Do you have eyes and fail to see . . . ? Well, yes and no. He was talking specifically to those who had witnessed the feeding of the multitude, asking whether they were willing to believe what their eyes were telling them, but his words apply equally to life in general. Are we ready to take a second look at the commonplace and familiar? Are we ready to open our eyes to what God wants to show us rather than to what we want to see? Are we ready to see the whole picture instead of just a tiny part. So much around us speaks of God's creative purpose and care for all. There's the beauty of the natural world, so full of interest and wonder. There's the evidence of lives transformed by the love of Christ. There are reminders of God's faithfulness in times past. There are deeds of kindness and compassion, and examples of faith and courage. And then, of course, there are situations of human need that call us to respond in his name . . . and so we could go on. If we could only learn to look more closely, we would recognise God's presence more often and see his hand at work more clearly.

Let us pause now and listen to celebrated words by the poet W. H. Davies (*read poem,* see above), reminding us of the need to stop, stare and reflect. After that, a selection of familiar items will be brought forward, one by one, in silence. Look carefully and ask yourself what each means, and what God is saying to you through them.

Prayers   *Praise*
Caring and compassionate God,
    for the knowledge that you are there –
    present among us,
    ready to listen,
    eager to respond –
    receive our praise,
    in the name of Christ.

For the knowledge that you are with us everywhere –
    ever-faithful,
    always true,
    unfailingly constant –
    receive our praise,
    in the name of Christ.

For the knowledge that, even when you seem distant, you are there –
    watching over us,
    equipping,
    enabling –
    receive our praise,
    in the name of Christ.

For the knowledge that, though we fail you, *you* will never fail us –
   your forgiveness free,
   complete,
   inexhaustible –
   receive our praise,
   in the name of Christ.
Amen.

Thanksgiving
Sovereign God,
   for everything that highlights your power,
   we thank you.

For everything that testifies to your purpose,
   we thank you.

For everything that illustrates your mercy,
   we thank you.

For everything that confirms your care,
   we thank you.

For everything that imparts your peace,
   we thank you.

For everything that reveals your goodness,
   we thank you.

For everything that demonstrates your grace,
   we thank you.

For everything that displays your love,
   we thank you.

For so much, O God, that points to you,
   we thank you.

In Christ's name we pray.
Amen.

Confession
Merciful God,
   we speak of faith,
   commitment,
   discipleship,
   yet all too often we live with little thought of you,
   forgetful of your presence
   and oblivious to your prompting.
For overlooking you in so much,
   forgive us, O Lord.

We wonder why sometimes you seem distant,
   why prayers appear to be unanswered,
   why faith no longer sparkles,
   when all the time you are there,
   responding in love,
   yearning to nurture,
   if only we would look and see.
For overlooking you in so much,
   forgive us, O Lord.

We ask you for help,
   strength,
   guidance,
   yet fail to recognise when you respond,
   either looking for the wrong answers
   or taking for granted the resources you put at our disposal.
For overlooking you in so much,
   forgive us, O Lord.

We pray to know you better,
   to be more like you
   and to grow in grace,
   yet repeatedly we are too busy to make proper time for you,
   too distracted by other interests and concerns,
   too preoccupied with self to think of anything else.
For overlooking you in so much,
   forgive us, O Lord.

Merciful God,
   open our eyes,
   our minds,
   our hearts
   and our souls –
   our lives in every part –
   to all the ways you speak and act,
   and so may we live each moment conscious of your nearness
   and rejoicing in your presence,
   through Jesus Christ our Lord.
Amen.

Intercession
Eternal God,
   hear our prayer for all those who cannot or will not see you,
   or who long to see you better.
Draw near,
   and reveal the breadth of your love to all.

We pray for those who have closed their minds to you,
  refusing to admit the possibility even of your existence.
Draw near,
  and reveal the breadth of your love to all.

We pray for those plagued by doubts and questions,
  wanting to believe
  but unable to see past the obstacles these present to faith.
Draw near,
  and reveal the breadth of your love to all.

We pray for those who lost their faith,
  no longer inspired by a sense of your nearness.
Draw near,
  and reveal the breadth of your love to all.

We pray for those who are young in faith,
  seeking to know and love you better.
Draw near,
  and reveal the breadth of your love to all.

We pray for those whose faith is long established,
  perhaps to the point that it has grown stale or jaded.
Draw near,
  and reveal the breadth of your love to all.

We pray for those whose lives have been overshadowed by sorrow,
  grief obscuring your continuing presence.
Draw near,
  and reveal the breadth of your love to all.

We pray for those whose lives are blighted by injustice and exploitation,
  any sign of your involvement in their lives hard to see.
Draw near,
  and reveal the breadth of your love to all.

We pray for those afflicted by suffering,
  pain of body, mind or spirit blotting out all else.
Draw near,
  and reveal the breadth of your love to all.

We pray for those in lands torn by war, violence and bloodshed,
  so much around them seeming to deny your purpose.
Draw near,
  and reveal the breadth of your love to all.

Eternal God,
    we look to a time when every knee will bow
    and every tongue confess your greatness.
Until then, we ask:
Draw near,
    and reveal the breadth of your love to all.
Amen.

Closing prayer
Gracious God,
    go with us on our way,
    and open our eyes whenever we lose sight of your presence.
Show us the way to walk,
    the way to serve
    and the way to know you better,
    through Jesus Christ our Lord.
Amen.

Order of Service

- Key verse
- Introduction
- Hymn
- Prayer of praise
- Quiz (1)
- Reading
- Quiz (2)
- Prayer of thanksgiving
- Hymn
- Talk
- Poem: 'Leisure'
- Silent procession and presentation of visual aids
- Hymn
- Prayer of confession
- Quiz (3)
- Prayer of intercession
- Hymn
- Closing prayer

5   Down Memory Lane

A family service using pictures and photographs

The aim of this service is to celebrate God's faithfulness in times past and so to build trust for the future.

Key verses

The enduring love of the Lord never fades, his mercies can never be exhausted; each morning they are made new, such is his great faithfulness. 'The Lord is all I need,' declares my soul, 'and so I will trust in him.'
Lamentations 3:22-24

Resources

- Slides/photographs/PowerPoint presentation of your village/town/city in 'the old days'.
- Slides/photographs/PowerPoint presentation of past members of your church.
- Memorabilia connected to your village/town/city and church.
- Video footage of events in last century.
- Anecdotes/brief reminiscences from members concerning past events.

Suggested music

- *Yesterday* (The Beatles)
- *Memories are made of this* (covered by numerous artists)
- *The way we were* (Barbra Streisand)

Suggested hymns

- Great is thy faithfulness
- Thy hand, O God, has guided
- Lord, for the years
- Our God, our help in ages past
- Rock of ages
- For all the love that from our earliest days

Introduction

'Do this in remembrance of me.' Those words from the Lord's Supper stand at the heart both of worship and of the Christian faith. But it's not just at Holy Communion that we are called to remember, nor is it simply the dying and rising of Christ we are urged to recall. For the Christian, remembering what God has done is part of the very fabric of life, pivotal to discipleship, for so often it is the example of former generations, the wisdom they have handed down, and the faithfulness of God that we, with them, have experienced that gives reassurance in the present and hope for the future. We come, then, today to celebrate the part that memories play in our lives, to give thanks for them and to celebrate all God has done and has yet to do.

Suggested readings

- Deuteronomy 11:18-25
- Ecclesiastes 12:1-8
- 1 Corinthians 11:23-26

Talk précis

Remember what God has done for you. Remember his faithfulness in times past. Remember the way he brought deliverance from Egypt and guidance during the long years in the wilderness. That message was imprinted on the people of Israel from their earliest days, passed on from generation to generation, recalled day after day, year after year with glad thanksgiving. It runs like a golden thread through the book of Deuteronomy (7:18; 8:2; 15:15; 16:3, 12; 24:9) and, similarly, through the Psalms (44:1-3; 89:1-4; 90:1-2; 105:5; 145:1-13). Theirs was a God who had set them free from captivity, guided them into the Promised Land, and watched over them throughout their subsequent history, the memory of his great goodness and faithful guidance across the years sustaining, enriching and feeding their faith. That God, of course, is our God too, and for us as Christians remembering has an equally special place. 'Do this in memory of me,' said Jesus (1 Corinthians 11:24). Such words remind us that our faith is not based on wishful thinking or idle speculation, nor on some clever deception or well-intentioned philosophy, but is rather rooted in history, in what God has done. Don't forget that. Make time to reflect on and recall his faithfulness across the ages: to his people of old, his Church, and to you. Remember what God has done, and in the light of that celebrate what he is doing now and look forward to all he is yet to do.

Prayers

Praise
Eternal God,
    for your involvement in human history –
    identifying yourself with the life of our world,
    active and interested in the daily affairs of life –
    in awe and wonder
    we praise you.

For the way you fashioned humankind in your image,
    calling, prompting and guiding from earliest times,
    seeking to lead us into a deeper knowledge of you
    and a more meaningful relationship,
    in awe and wonder
    we praise you.

For calling Abram to venture into the unknown,
    Moses to lead your people out of captivity,
    kings and judges to rule over your people
    and prophets to proclaim your word,
    in awe and wonder
    we praise you.

For sharing our humanity in Christ,
   walking our earth,
   sharing our joys and sorrows,
   hopes and fears,
   life and death,
   in awe and wonder
   we praise you.

For your victory over death,
   the rekindling of faith among the Apostles,
   the birth of your Church
   and the gift of your Spirit,
   in awe and wonder
   we praise you.

For generations since,
   witnesses across the centuries,
   lives committed to you,
   discipleship offered faithfully in the service of Christ,
   in awe and wonder
   we praise you.

For those we have known and loved,
   who have been part of *our* story,
   capturing our imagination and firing our faith,
   offering encouragement,
   inspiration,
   support
   and guidance,
   in awe and wonder
   we praise you.

Eternal God,
   for all we have to look back on,
   to remember,
   to celebrate
   and learn from,
   in awe and wonder
   we praise you.

In the name of Christ.
Amen.

Thanksgiving
For memories of special occasions,
   God of past, present and future,
   gladly we thank you.

For memories of special people,
   God of past, present and future,
     gladly we thank you.

For memories of special places,
   God of past, present and future,
     gladly we thank you.

For memories of special achievements,
   God of past, present and future,
     gladly we thank you.

For memories of special blessing,
   God of past, present and future,
     gladly we thank you.

For memories of special guidance,
   God of past, present and future,
     gladly we thank you.

For all the events and experiences
   that have gladdened our lives in any way,
   God of past, present and future,
     gladly we thank you.
Amen.

Confession
Loving God,
   despite all you have done for us
   we do not always remember your goodness –
   the many reasons we have to celebrate,
   the innumerable blessings for which we should give thanks;
   in fact, all too often, we forget what you have given.
For taking so much for granted,
   forgive us.

Despite the ways you have led us across the years –
   the moments you have helped us in times of need,
   the times you have spoken through your word,
   the experiences through which we have glimpsed your hand at work –
   we have failed to recall all we owe you,
   repeatedly overlooking your unfailing provision.
For taking so much for granted,
   forgive us.

Despite the treasures we've received,
   the joys we've experienced,
   the love we've shared
   and the plenty we've enjoyed,
   we have been preoccupied with what we may yet acquire,
   hankering after more rather than celebrating what we have.
For taking so much for granted,
   forgive us.

Loving God,
   despite your faithfulness in so much,
   your willingness to forgive and go on forgiving,
   your constant and unfailing love,
   we have been faithless,
   careless in discipleship
   and weak in commitment.
For taking so much for granted,
   forgive us.
Amen.

Intercession
Sovereign God,
   we pray for those whose memories are painful,
   causing grief,
   revulsion,
   regret
   or despair.
Bring healing,
   bring hope.

We pray for victims of violence,
   crime,
   abuse
   and cruelty –
   all who carry deep within the scars of past wrongs.
Bring healing,
   bring hope.

We pray for those who have suffered break-ups in relationships,
   aching to recapture times long gone,
   yearning for the companionship of a partner,
   children,
   parents
   or friends.
Bring healing,
   bring hope.

We pray for those wrestling with old age,
    looking back wistfully to days of health and strength,
    hope and promise,
    happy memories tinged with sadness.
Bring healing,
    bring hope.

We pray for those scarred by memories of war and conflict,
    haunted by images of hatred and brutality –
    those who long to forget yet find themselves unable to do so,
    their recollections too vivid,
    reality too stark.
Bring healing,
    bring hope.

We pray for those who are bereaved,
    all who mourn loved ones,
    their memory bringing pleasure, yet pain,
    laughter, yet tears,
    and grief sometimes overwhelming in its intensity.
Bring healing,
    bring hope.

Sovereign God,
    hear our prayer for all,
    in the name of Christ.
Amen.

Closing prayer
Faithful God,
    teach us,
    today and always,
    to live in the light of all you have done:
    the love you have so faithfully shown,
    guidance so faithfully given,
    promises so faithfully fulfilled
    and blessings so faithfully offered.
Teach us,
    remembering such constancy,
    to celebrate the present
    and trust you for the future,
    through Jesus Christ our Lord.
Amen.

Order of Service

- Slide/PowerPoint presentations can be supplemented by backing music (see *Suggested music* on page 40).
- Music
- Key verses
- Introduction
- Prayer of praise
- Hymn
- Slide/PowerPoint presentation
- Reading
- Prayer of thanksgiving
- Hymn
- Personal reminiscences
- Viewing of memorabilia
- Slide/PowerPoint or video presentation
- Prayer of confession
- Hymn
- Reading
- Talk
- Prayer of intercession
- Hymn
- Blessing
- Closing prayer

SOUND

6   The sound of silence

A service exploring the gift of quietness

The aim of this service is to recognise the importance of stillness and quietness in the presence of God, and to offer such a time as a pattern for future devotion.

Key verse

Be still and know that I am God.
Psalm 46:10

Resources

- The main resource you need for this service is times of silence. It sounds simple, but it's harder to allow substantial times of quiet than you might imagine! You may also want to make selective use of the suggested music listed below.

Suggested music

- *The sound of silence* (Simon and Garfunkel)
- *Silence is golden* (The Tremeloes)
- *Moonlight Sonata* (Beethoven); first movement
- 'Meditation' from *Thaïs* (Massenet)

Suggested hymns

- Let all mortal flesh keep silence
- Be still for the presence of the Lord
- Peace is flowing like a river
- Be still and know that I am God
- The peace of the earth be with you
- Be still, my soul
- Peace before us
- Father of peace, and God of love
- Lord of all hopefulness
- Peace, perfect peace, in this dark world of sin
- Give me peace, O Lord
- Go peaceful, in gentleness
- Lord, I lift my hands to you in prayer
- Peace, perfect peace, is the gift
- Peace to you

Introduction

When did you last set aside quiet time for personal devotion outside of Sunday worship? How often do you pause to reflect, to act on those words 'Be still and know that I am God'? For most of us it's probably been longer than we'd like to admit and longer than we know it should be. It's not that we mean to neglect such times, simply that there is always so much else clamouring for our attention. Yet, however valid our excuse might be, deep down we know that our lives are impoverished as a result and our discipleship weakened.

Today, we set aside time not simply to think about silence but to celebrate it, seeking quietness of mind and tranquillity of spirit not just for us but for all.

Suggested readings

- 1 Kings 19:1-13
- Psalm 46:1-11

Talk précis

According to psychologists, our lives today are short of silence. Some people, we are told, are almost frightened of it, switching on the radio or television rather than be alone for a few moments with their thoughts. Whether that's true or not I'll leave with you, but it's certainly the case that the busy schedule of life can make it hard sometimes to snatch a few moments in which to be still and reflect. Need that matter? Not necessarily, for God is able to speak as much through the hurly-burly of our daily routine as through moments set aside for him; indeed, some might say more so. Yet, true though that is, quiet times can provide an important counterbalance, preventing us from being swept along unthinkingly by the current of events – something that can happen all too easily. Furthermore, though God *can* speak within the bustle of a busy day, most of us will know from experience that he can equally easily be crowded out so that we scarcely give him a second thought.

'Be still and know that I am God' – that advice is given for a reason, for God recognises as much as any how simple it is to lose sight of his presence. If we are to recognise his presence and allow him to speak, then we need times set apart to focus on him so that he can direct our thoughts, such times enabling us to consecrate every moment and to return to the fray with a new perspective, a fresh awareness of God's involvement in it all.

For the prophet Elijah an experience like that came on Mount Horeb, catching him completely by surprise. First there came a mighty wind, then an earthquake, then fire – each at the time seen as signs of God's presence but, more important for our purposes, each also associated with noise, energy, movement, furious activity. Is this God, thinks Elijah? It must be. But it's not, God finally making himself known instead in a still small voice, a gentle whisper, the sound of silence. And in that moment, the turmoil Elijah was experiencing in his own life, and the chaos of the world around him, was suddenly resolved, finding a place within the purpose and love of God.

Make room yourselves for that still small voice in worship, that sound of silence in your own devotions. Yes, words are important too, allowing us to voice our praise, articulate our gratitude, acknowledge our mistakes and express our concern for others; yes, music and song can equally capture our imagination, speaking both *for* and *to* us; but lose sight of the importance of quietness and the chances are we may lose sight of God as well.

Prayers   *Praise*
Mighty God,
    so often and so easily we bombard you with words,
    afraid that if we are not speaking
    we are not praying,
    but today we make time for silence,
    to be still and know that you are God.

Silence

There are no words sufficient to express your greatness.
In silent homage
    we worship you.

Silence

You are above all,
    before all,
    beyond all.
In silent homage
    we worship you.

Silence

Your ways are not our ways,
    neither are your thoughts our thoughts.
In silent homage
    we worship you.

Silence

We have no claim on your goodness,
    no virtue that can earn your love,
    yet you want us to know you
    even as we are fully known.
In silent homage
    we worship you.

Silence

Language fails us in your presence,
    but we would meet with you
    and have you meet with us,
    so that in all we say and do and are
    we might truly honour you.
In silent homage
    we worship you.

Silence

Mighty God,
 we bring you our words,
 we bring you our silence,
 in the name of Christ.
Amen.

Thanksgiving

God of peace,
 with heartfelt gratitude we celebrate the quiet moments in our lives –
 opportunities to pause and ponder,
 stop and stare,
 relax and reflect.
For all such moments mean,
 we thank you, O Lord.

We celebrate breaks in the busy routine of life –
 times when the pressures ease,
 the responsibilities lessen
 and the workload is lightened.
For all such moments mean,
 we thank you, O Lord.

We celebrate times of tranquillity –
 the stillness of the sky at night,
 the sound of birds singing,
 the view from a mountaintop,
 the gentle murmur of a stream –
 so much in this world you have given
 bringing quietness to the spirit
 and rest to the mind.
For all such moments mean,
 we thank you, O Lord.

We celebrate moments set aside from the bustle of each day –
 times of worship,
 retreat,
 meditation
 and personal devotion.
For all such moments mean,
 we thank you, O Lord.

We celebrate the calm we can feel even in the fiercest storm –
 the inner confidence that you will meet our needs
 and see us through,
 nothing in either life or death finally able to separate us
 from your love in Christ.
For all such moments mean,
 we thank you, O Lord.

Gratefully we come,
   gratefully we worship,
   gratefully we celebrate your gift of peace,
   in the name of Christ.
Amen.

Confession
Gentle God,
   we have squandered the peace you give us.
Forgive us,
   and bring rest to our souls once more.

We have failed to be still in your presence,
   to know, simply, that you are our God.
Forgive us,
   and bring rest to our souls once more.

We have neglected worship and been careless in devotion,
   denying ourselves the resources you long to give.
Forgive us,
   and bring rest to our souls once more.

We have disobeyed your word and ignored your guidance,
   shutting you out of our lives.
Forgive us,
   and bring rest to our souls once more.

We have failed to take stock of our lives,
   to examine ourselves as we should.
Forgive us,
   and bring rest to our souls once more.

We have brooded over what we cannot change
   instead of placing our troubles in your hands.
Forgive us,
   and bring rest to our souls once more.

We have filled our lives with trivia,
   rushing from one thing to another but ignoring what matters most.
Forgive us,
   and bring rest to our souls once more.

We have turned in on self and our own interests,
   forgetting that liberation lies in letting go.
Forgive us,
   and bring rest to our souls once more.

For proclaiming peace that passes understanding
    yet so often throwing that most precious gift away,
    we come, Lord, in penitence.
Forgive us,
    and bring rest to our souls once more.

In Christ's name we pray.
Amen.

Intercession
Gentle and gracious God,
    we pray for those who, even in times of silence,
    know no sense of inner calm,
    no quietness of mind,
    no tranquillity of spirit.
Still their restless souls,
    and grant your peace that passes understanding.

We pray for those troubled by fears,
    phobias,
    anxieties
    and uncertainty,
    unable to escape from terrors, real or imagined.
Still their restless souls,
    and grant your peace that passes understanding.

We pray for those trapped in the rat race,
    with no time to stop and stare,
    to take stock of what really matters,
    to reflect on who they are and what life is all about.
Still their restless souls,
    and grant your peace that passes understanding.

We pray for those tormented by regrets,
    disappointments,
    hurts
    and frustration,
    their enjoyment of life undermined by bitterness, envy and resentment.
Still their restless souls,
    and grant your peace that passes understanding.

We pray for those in lands ravaged by war,
    caught up in a cycle of hatred,
    suspicion,
    violence
    and slaughter.
Still their restless souls,
    and grant your peace that passes understanding.

We pray for those living in the shadow of death –
    troubled at the prospect of dying,
    mourning loved ones
    or fearful for the safety of loved ones.
Still their restless souls,
    and grant your peace that passes understanding.

To all those whose minds are in turmoil,
    and lives in chaos,
    bring your gentle touch,
    an inner calm and tranquillity even in the fiercest storm.
Still their restless souls,
    and grant your peace that passes understanding.

In Christ's name we pray.
Amen.

Closing prayer
Deep peace of the running wave,
deep peace of the flowing air,
deep peace of the quiet earth,
deep peace of the shining stars,
deep peace of the Son of Peace,
be with you for ever.
Celtic blessing

Order of Service

Times of silence need to be long enough to be significant but not so long that people become uncomfortable or their attention starts to stray. You will find that even a few minutes seems a surprisingly long time.

- Music
- Key verse
- Introduction
- Prayer of praise
- Hymn
- Reading: Psalm
- Silent reflection
- Poem: 'Leisure' (see page 33)
- Silent reflection
- Music
- Silent reflection
- Hymn
- Reading
- Silent reflection
- Prayer of thanksgiving
- Hymn
- Talk
- Silent reflection
- Prayer of confession
- Hymn
- Silent reflection
- Prayer of intercession
- Hymn
- Closing prayer

7 Who said that?

A fun family service exploring the way God speaks today

The aim of this service is to ask whether we can recognise people's voices, and whether we can recognise when God is speaking to us.

Key verse

He asked, 'Who are you, Lord?'
Acts 9:5a

Resources

- For this service you will need to record brief snippets of people talking. Aim for a varied selection, including voices of celebrities/ newsreaders/commentators recorded from the radio, television, videos, DVDs, etc., and those of members of your congregation. Ensure that your recording and the amplification system you will use during the service are of sufficient quality that people can hear clearly throughout the church building.

Suggested hymns

- Listen, let your heart keep seeking
- Master, speak! Thy servant heareth
- Lord, speak to me
- O Lord of life, thy quickening voice
- I heard the voice of Jesus say
- Jesus is Lord! Creation's voice proclaims it
- Lord, today your voice is calling
- God has spoken – by the prophets

Introduction

Our service today revolves around voices, some familiar and others perhaps not so familiar. We will be listening to various recordings and asking which voice we recognise and which we don't. There are no prizes for getting them right and there's no shame in getting them wrong; it's just a light-hearted bit of fun, but fun with a purpose, for we will be exploring through it the ways God might speak to us, specifically through others, and asking whether we are ready to recognise his voice when he speaks.

Suggested readings

- 1 Samuel 3:1-21
- Acts 9:1-19a

Talk précis

Have you ever had the experience of hearing a voice on the radio but not quite being able to place it? I'm sure you have, and if so you'll know how maddening it can be. You can almost picture the person's face – the time you heard them last, or a scene in which they featured – almost, but not quite. The puzzle niggles away at you until you finally crack it, at last managing to put a face to the voice, a name to the sound.

With God, the analogy quickly breaks down, for, much though we would like to, few if any of us would claim ever to hear an unmistakable voice from heaven; indeed, if we claimed to do so many would seriously question our sanity. Yet though God rarely speaks directly, we nonetheless often sense a call, challenge or summons, a message of hope, guidance or reassurance, even if we can't quite always place where it comes from. Sometimes it is evidently of God – a passage in Scripture, or words in a sermon or prayer; at other times God is less obviously present, speaking perhaps through the words of family, friends, colleagues at work or even a complete stranger. The voices may be familiar or unfamiliar, but through them God can be calling, for so often he uses ordinary people and everyday situations to speak for him.

So it was for Samuel in our first reading and Paul in our second. Yes, at first sight they seem to have had the sort of special audience with God that we were saying earlier is all too rare, but look more closely, for in Samuel's case Eli heard nothing, and in Paul's those with him on the road to Damascus heard a sound but did not recognise it as God speaking. Furthermore, it took Eli to recognise that God was calling Samuel, and Ananias to help Paul recognise what God was saying; in one case the voice of a friend and in the other the voice of a stranger. And each having been alerted to his call, God was able to speak to others through them in turn.

Are you listening in vain for God's guidance? Are you wondering why he fails to answer your prayers? Are you hungry to hear his voice? Then maybe you need to listen more closely to those around you, or the words of Scripture, or the words of others across the years. Maybe God has been speaking all the time, only we have failed to listen or recognise his voice.

Prayers

Praise and thanksgiving

Eternal God,
    we celebrate today the way you have spoken across the ages,
    calling,
    guiding,
    rebuking,
    inspiring –
    proclaiming your word of truth,
    grace,
    love
    and life.
For still speaking today,
    Lord, we praise you.

We celebrate the way you have spoken across the world,
    the message of the gospel touching the hearts of people

from every continent and every walk of life –
East and West,
North and South,
male and female,
rich and poor –
your word heard in a multitude of places
in a multitude of ways.
For still speaking today,
Lord, we praise you.

We celebrate the way you have spoken
despite every attempt to silence you,
your voice refusing to be stifled –
confronting darkness,
calling for justice,
and conquering hatred with love,
evil with good.
For still speaking today,
Lord, we praise you.

We celebrate the way you have spoken in so many different ways:
through the testimony of prophets,
the person of Christ,
the prompting of the Spirit,
the fellowship of your people,
the preaching of your word,
the sharing of worship,
the world around us,
the vastness of the universe
and the daily events of life.
For still speaking today,
Lord, we praise you.

Eternal God,
receive our worship,
our homage,
our adoration,
and speak afresh now,
through Jesus Christ our Lord.
Amen.

Confession
For resisting your voice,
not liking what we hear,
gracious God
forgive us.

For ignoring your voice,
    preferring our way to yours,
    gracious God
    forgive us.

For mistaking your voice,
    confusing it with the beguiling tones of this world,
    gracious God
    forgive us.

For suppressing your voice,
    drowning it out with the noise of daily bustle,
    gracious God
    forgive us.

For silencing your voice,
    living in a way that prevents you speaking through us,
    gracious God
    forgive us.

For distorting your voice,
    twisting it according to our expectations,
    gracious God
    forgive us.

For restricting your voice,
    allowing prejudices and preconceptions to close our ears,
    gracious God
    forgive us.

For missing your voice,
    failing to recognise it speaking all around us,
    gracious God
    forgive us.

For all the ways we fail to hear you
    or fail to listen,
    gracious God
    forgive us.
Amen.

Intercession
Loving God,
    for all who call out to you,
    longing to hear your voice of comfort,
    reassurance,
    inspiration
    and guidance,

we bring our prayer.
May your word bring help,
   your voice give hope.

We pray for those who feel lost,
   life seeming to be devoid of meaning,
   whatever they turn to in their quest for happiness
   somehow never offering the fulfilment they seek.
May your word bring help,
   your voice give hope.

We pray for those wrestling with chronic pain,
   debilitating disease
   or terminal illness,
   crying out for relief,
   yearning for healing,
   struggling to reconcile their experience with their faith in you.
May your word bring help,
   your voice give hope.

We pray for those enduring mental anguish –
   struggling with depression,
   coping with divorce or other breakdowns in relationships,
   oppressed by real or imagined fears,
   crushed by bereavement,
May your word bring help,
   your voice give hope.

We pray for those suffering deprivation –
   the poor,
   homeless
   and unemployed;
   all in our own country who feel trapped by circumstances,
   denied a stake in society.
May your word bring help,
   your voice give hope.

We pray for the millions in abject poverty across the world,
   denied the essentials we take for granted,
   deprived of resources to help themselves,
   defeated by market forces beyond their control.
May your word bring help,
   your voice give hope.

We pray for those in lands broken by war –
   scarred by brutality,
   ravaged by hatred
   and engulfed by fear.

May your word bring help,
    your voice give hope.

Loving God,
    speak into each and every situation,
    and, by your grace,
    bring guidance,
    succour,
    tranquillity,
    opportunity,
    provision
    and peace.
May your word bring help,
    your voice give hope.

In Christ's name we ask it.
Amen.

Closing prayer
As you have spoken here, Lord,
    speak everywhere.
Go with us now
    and teach us to listen for your voice,
    wherever it might be
    and however you might speak,
    so that we may know you by our sides,
    this day
    and always.
Amen.

Order of Service

- Key verse
- Introduction
- Hymn
- Prayer of praise and thanksgiving
- Voices quiz (1)
- Reading
- Voices quiz (2)
- Hymn
- Reading
- Talk
- Prayer of confession
- Hymn
- Prayer of intercession
- Hymn
- Closing prayer

8   Thank you for the music

An act of worship using recorded music

The aim of this service is to recognise and celebrate the power of music in expressing our thoughts and feelings in worship, and thus to give a reminder that prayer need not always be confined to the spoken word.

Key verses

Praise the Lord! Sing a new song to him, offer praise among the congregation of his people. Let Israel exult in its Maker, the children of Zion celebrate their King, praising his name as they dance and making melody to him through tambourine and lyre.
Psalm 149:1-3

Resources

- For this talk you will need a selection of recorded music (classical, pop, or a mixture of both), chosen to reflect different moods/aspects of worship. Much classical music was written with a religious aim or context in mind, and so lends itself naturally to the context of worship, but, carefully chosen, other music can be equally appropriate. Ensure you have a good amplification system, giving undistorted sound quality throughout the church building. You may also need to check copyright before playing recorded tracks.

Suggested music

As indicated above, music is intended to replace the spoken word in prayer during this service (though I have included brief introductory and closing prayers). Music suggestions are therefore given under *Prayers* (see below), arranged under the four headings: *Praise*, *Confession*, *Thanksgiving* and *Intercession* (most of the songs under *Intercession* can be downloaded free, under licence, over the Internet).

Suggested hymns

- For the music of creation
- Come, let us join our cheerful songs
- When the music fades
- Make a joyful noise, all ye people
- Shout for joy and sing
- Born in song!
- I will sing your praises

Introduction

What's new, you might think, about a music service? Most churches will have made time for an occasional 'songs of praise' celebration, and many will have given opportunities for musical gifts within the congregation to be recognised and offered to God. Even if we don't do that, music is still key to our worship, whether through a choir or music group, an organ or piano, a guitar or keyboard. Today, though, we do something slightly different, using music not just as an accompaniment or an element of worship, but placing it at the very centre, using pieces carefully chosen to express our response to God in praise, confession, thanksgiving and intercession. Come, then, to celebrate all that music offers, but above all to make music in your hearts, to sing a new song, and in a way beyond words to respond to the presence of God among us.

Suggested readings

- 1 Chronicles 15:16-28
- Psalm 149:1-5; 150
- Ephesians 3:15-20

Talk précis

Which elements in a typical Sunday service most help you worship God? Some might highlight the reading of Scripture, others the sermon, others again the prayers, and others still the Lord's Supper, and no doubt we've all found each of these immensely meaningful at times in our lives, but probably equally important, though we may not fully realise it, is music. The first thing many do when they enter church is look up the hymns to see whether they know and like them. In some services the choir plays a central role, in others it's the music group, and imagine how little atmosphere there would be if instead of music before and after worship there was simply silence. Across the centuries, music has found a key place in worship, right back to Old Testament times: 'David, together with all the people of Israel, celebrated exuberantly before the Lord, singing and making music with harps, lyres, cymbals and trumpets . . . The Israelites brought the ark of the covenant up to the accompaniment of ram's horns and trumpets, cymbals, lyres and harps' (1 Chronicles 13:8; 15:28). Similar sentiments are found in Psalms 149 and 150: 'Sing a new song to the Lord, sing his praises among the congregation of the faithful. Let Zion's people rejoice in their king, praising his name, dancing and making music upon the harp and tambourine. For the Lord delights in his people and honours the humble with salvation. Let the faithful exult in this privilege and sing jubilantly on their beds' (Psalm 149:1-5). Indeed, in the Psalms we see songs expressing all kinds of emotions: joy and sorrow, hope and fear, faith and doubt, confidence and despair, to name but some. The same has been true of much music written across the centuries, including some of that we've heard today; written in response to God, expressing similar thoughts and feelings. And so it is also with the hymns we sing week by week, these articulating in their turn joy, celebration, thanksgiving, confession, petition, intercession and so much more – music for just about every occasion, every aspect of worship.

Today we have recognised afresh all that music offers and thanked God for it, but, more than that, we have recognised how it can speak for us in expressing our response to everything God has done. Remember that, and you will find music to be not just a pleasing accompaniment to worship, but worship itself.

Prayers

Opening prayer
Loving God,
    we have come to celebrate your gift of music –
    to let it speak *to* us
    and *for* us,
    expressing our joy and praise,
    articulating our sorrow at our faults and faithlessness,
    offering our gratitude for your many blessings
    and conveying our concern
    for the innumerable needs within our world.
Help us, as we listen,
    not just to enjoy
    but also to worship
    and to pray,
    sensing your presence,
    opening our lives to your prompting
    and committing ourselves to your service.
In Christ's name we ask it.
Amen.

Praise
- 'Gloria' from *Gloria* (Vivaldi)
- 'The heavens are telling' from *The Creation* (Haydn)
- 'Laudamus te' from *Mass in C Minor* (Mozart)
- *O for the wings of a dove* (Mendelssohn)
- *Panis Angelicus* (Franck)
- *O Magnum Mysterium* (Palestrina)
- 'Adoramus te' from *Fountain of Life* (Margaret Rizza)
- 'Praise God, all Christians' from *Magnificat* (Praetorius)

Confession
- 'Kyrie eleison' from *Requiem* (Mozart)
- *Miserere mei* (Allegri)
- 'Pié Jesu' from *Requiem* (Andrew Lloyd Webber)
- 'Have mercy, O Lord' from *St Matthew's Passion* (J. S. Bach)
- 'Kyrie eleison' from *Fountain of Life* (Margaret Rizza)

Thanksgiving
- *What a wonderful world* (Louis Armstrong)
- 'Gratias' from *Requiem* (Mozart)
- 'Pilgrims' Chorus' from *Tannhaüser* (Wagner)

Intercession
- *I'd like to teach the world to sing* (The New Seekers)
- *Scarecrow* (Melissa Everidge)
- *Streets of London* (Ralph McTell)
- *Give peace a chance* (John Lennon)
- *Imagine* (John Lennon)
- *Touch the world* (Earth, Wind and Fire)
- *We are the world* (USA for Africa)
- *Have a little faith in me* (John Hiatt)
- *Let love rule* (Lenny Kravitz)

Closing prayer
Gracious God,
    as we have offered music to you in worship
    and asked you to speak to us through it,
    so now may we go out into the world
    and back to our daily business,
    with a song on our lips
    and a joyful noise welling up in our hearts,
    living each day with thanksgiving
    and each moment with love,
    until that day when,
    with the great company of heaven,
    we lift up our voices in praise
    and exult for ever, with all creation, in your presence.
Amen.

Order of Service

Remember that the medium of prayer in this service is music; avoid the temptation to add words.

- Key verses
- Introduction
- Opening prayer
- Hymn
- Reading
- Prayer of praise (see *Prayers* above)
- Scripture verse
- Prayer of confession (see *Prayers* above)
- Scripture verse
- Hymn
- Reading
- Prayer of thanksgiving (see *Prayers* above)
- Reading
- Talk
- Hymn
- Prayer of intercession (see *Prayers* above)
- Scripture verse
- Closing prayer

9   Ears to hear

*A time of reflection using recorded sounds
of the world around us*

The aim of this service is to celebrate the gift of hearing and to point to the way that God can speak through the ordinary sounds of life if we are ready to listen. (You will need to use the material sensitively should your congregation include those who are aurally impaired.)

Key verse

The hearing ear and the seeing eye, God has made them both.
Proverbs 20:12

Morning after morning he awakens me – he wakens my ear to listen to what he would teach me.
Isaiah 50:4b-5

Do you have ears yet fail to hear . . . ?
Mark 8:18b

Resources

- For this service you will need recorded snippets of the everyday things we hear around us (for example, a dog barking, aeroplane passing, water dripping, baby crying, person walking, bird singing, clock ticking, car passing, train hooting, children playing). If you record these yourself, you will need high-quality recording equipment to prevent hiss and sound distortion. You will find it easier and faster to download sound effects off the Internet. Sites providing free downloads include http://www.prankcallsunlimited.com/freesoundeffects.htm and http://www.a1freesoundeffects.com. Try to achieve a balanced spread between sounds of nature and sounds of the town, city and home.
- As well as sound effects, you might also ask the congregation to be silent for a time and to listen carefully to all the sounds they can hear that they might not previously have noticed.

Suggested music

- *Clock Symphony* (Haydn)
- *Toy Symphony* (Haydn)
- *Cuckoo Polka* (Johann Strauss)
- *Voices of Spring* (Johann Strauss)

Suggested hymns

- O Lord, my God (How great thou art)
- Morning has broken
- Listen, let your heart keep seeking
- All things bright and beautiful
- Lord, you created a world full of splendour

- There's an awesome sound
- Listen, let your heart keep seeking
- Lord, speak to me
- O Lord of life, thy quickening voice
- Jesus is Lord! Creation's voice proclaims it

Introduction

How good are you at listening? No, I don't mean listening to others, though you may be very good at that. I mean listening to the world around you. How much do you hear of what's going on, and how much do you unconsciously blot out? The answer may surprise you, for much of the time there are all sorts of background noises as we go about our daily business that we barely register, either because they are so familiar that we have grown used to them or because we're engrossed in something else. There's nothing wrong in that, of course, but occasionally it pays to pause and consider some of the sounds we take for granted, for they remind us of the diversity and wonder of life, the rich variety God has given us to enjoy, each able to speak to us of God just as God is able to speak to us through them. We focus, then, today on the world of sound, so that we might perhaps be more open to God's voice everywhere around us, tomorrow and every day.

Suggested reading Psalm 19:1-4

Talk précis

Does God still speak today? We believe he does, of course, but in what ways? Most of us, I suspect, have often wished he spoke more clearly, in such a way that his voice is unmistakable and his wishes plain, but sadly life isn't like that. We don't hear a voice from on high. We don't have a direct line through to heaven. In fact, most of the time we have little if any sense of God speaking. But perhaps that's because we're expecting the wrong thing or looking in the wrong place. Think for a moment of those words of Jesus that run like a refrain through his teaching: 'All those who have ears to hear,' he urges his listeners (Matthew 11:15; 13:9, 43; Mark 4:9, 23; 7:16; Luke 8:8; 14:35), 'let them listen.' He means by that, of course, a lot of things – that we must be open to what we may not like to hear; that we must make time to reflect on his words; that we must be prepared to look beneath the surface sometimes to deeper meaning underneath – but is not contained within all that the idea that God can often be heard only if we are ready to listen? Did not Jesus himself repeatedly draw on illustrations from the natural world to show how so much within it speaks of him and his kingdom? The problem is that much can become so familiar that it passes us by, no longer speaking to us as it once did. Like the crowd after the feeding of the five thousand, we have ears yet fail to hear (Mark 8:18b). Today we have heard commonplace sounds, the sort of things we hear each and every day, yet to the ear of faith they speak of the wonder of life and of the God behind them. As the words of Psalm 19:1-4 put it, 'The heavens proclaim the glory of God; the universe testifies to his handi-work. Each day bears eloquent witness, and each night communicates knowledge, without need of speech, language or any other voice. Their music pervades all the earth, the words of their mouth reach out to the furthest parts of the world.'

Does God speak today? Yes, we believe so, and not just through words of Scripture, prayers or a sermon, the voice of conscience or voices of others; he speaks too through ordinary sounds around us, simple things we so often and easily take for granted. Those who have ears to hear, let them listen.

Prayers

Praise and thanksgiving
Almighty God,
   for the gift of sound
   and all we are able to hear around us,
   joyfully we worship you.

For the sound of the wind blowing in the trees,
   waves breaking on the shore,
   birds singing in the trees
   and water bubbling in a stream,
   Lord,
   we praise and thank you.

For the sound of geese calling,
   cattle lowing,
   sheep bleating
   and horses galloping,
   Lord,
   we praise and thank you.

For the sound of people talking,
   children playing,
   babies gurgling
   and crowds laughing,
   Lord,
   we praise and thank you.

For the sounds of town and cities,
   the hum of traffic,
   the buzz of conversation
   and the clatter of striding feet,
   Lord,
   we praise and thank you.

For the sound of a concert orchestra,
    a brass band,
    a jazz ensemble
    and a choir in song,
    Lord,
    we praise and thank you.

For the sound of rock 'n' roll,
    disco music,
    a ballad,
    a rap group,
    Lord,
    we praise and thank you.

For all this and so much more,
    and, above all, for the way you speak within it,
    Lord,
    we praise and thank you.
Amen.

Confession
Lord,
    you speak in so many ways,
    but we fail to hear it,
    our hearts not tuned to your voice.
Open our ears,
    open our lives,
    body, heart and soul.

We fail to hear the beauty in the simple sounds of nature,
    too busy to listen,
    or inured by familiarity to the wonder of it all.
Open our ears,
    open our lives,
    body, heart and soul.

We fail to hear the pain in a loved one's voice,
    too preoccupied with our own needs, desires or concerns
    to hear their mute appeal for help.
Open our ears,
    open our lives,
    body, heart and soul.

We fail to hear the cry of the poor,
    too selfish to recognise their voice
    calling through the newspaper report,
    the TV bulletin or the charity appeal.

Open our ears,
  open our lives,
  body, heart and soul.

We fail to hear your challenge in the voice of others,
    too set in our ways or full of our own ideas
    to recognise that we can learn from their experience,
    benefit from their insights.
Open our ears,
  open our lives,
  body, heart and soul.

We fail to hear your voice in the words of Scripture,
    too busy with other things to read it
    or too convinced that we know already what it has to say.
Open our ears,
  open our lives,
  body, heart and soul.

We fail to hear your voice within,
    too easily suppressing the voice of conscience,
    resisting the prompting of the Spirit,
    shying away from times of quietness
    in which your word might break through.
Open our ears,
  open our lives,
  body, heart and soul.

Lord,
    continue to speak
    and teach us to listen and learn.
Teach us, amid all the rich and varied sounds of life,
    to listen for your voice
    and, just as you always hear us,
    help us to hear you.
Amen.

Intercession
Loving God,
    we pray for those who cannot hear,
    who have to rely on sign language or touch
    to communicate with those around them.
Through your still small voice within,
    may your word assure them of your love and care.

We pray for the hard of hearing,
    often left out of conversations,
    mistaken for being slow,
    stupid,
    or uninterested in what is being said,
    yet in reality longing to hear,
    oppressed by a sense of isolation,
    and haunted by the prospect of a world of total silence.
Through your still small voice within,
    may your word assure them of your love and care.

We pray for those who, though hearing, will not or do not listen;
    closed to the voice of others,
    to the voice of nature
    and above all to your voice.
Through your still small voice within,
    may your word assure them of your love and care.

Finally we pray for those who have heard nothing of you –
    who have never had the gospel preached to them,
    never had the faith explained,
    never had the opportunity to respond.
Through your still small voice within,
    may your word assure them of your love and care.

All this we ask through Jesus Christ our Lord.
Amen.

Closing prayers

May the world continue to surprise us,
    love continue to astonish us,
    life continue to captivate us,
    faith continue to sustain us,
    and may God go with us always,
    now and for evermore.
Amen.

Ever-present God,
    as we return to the daily routine of life,
    awaken us to all the ways you might call,
    all the ways you might guide
    and all the ways you *do* speak,
    through Jesus Christ our Lord.
Amen.

Order of Service

- Key verse
- Introduction
- Hymn
- Prayer of praise and thanksgiving
- 'Sounds' quiz (1)
- Silent reflection
- 'Sounds' quiz (2)
- Reading
- Hymn
- Prayer of confession
- 'Sounds' quiz (3)
- Reading
- Talk
- Hymn
- Prayer of intercession
- Hymn
- Closing prayers

10   The language of love

A fun family service using different languages/dialects
to illustrate how love speaks across divides

The aim of this service is to emphasise the fact that love, and in particular the message of God's love in Christ, cuts across the things that keep us apart.

Key verse

My dear friends, given that God loves us so deeply, we should similarly love one another.
1 John 4:12

Resources

• This service makes use of different languages and dialects to illustrate the differences that make it hard for us to communicate with others. Specifically, it uses various well-known phrases spoken in foreign languages and in various UK accents/dialects (you could include Cockney rhyming slang and rap within this). If you are lucky enough to have people in your congregation fluent in foreign languages or with pronounced accents, then you can enlist their help in the service. Otherwise, you will need to make/borrow/hire recordings. If you choose the latter option, it may be that you could involve students at a local secondary school/college/university, thus encouraging interest there in the service. Numerous websites contain downloadable audio clips of European languages; for example: http://www.bbc.co.uk/kent/do_see/france/learn_french.shtml.

• On long sheets of paper, print off foreign language equivalents of various well-known phrases/expressions (but not those you will be using during the service!).

Suggested music

• *Love is a many splendoured thing* (covered by various artists)
• *All you need is love* (The Beatles)
• *The power of love* (Frankie Goes to Hollywood)

Suggested hymns

• Love divine, all love's excelling
• In heavenly love abiding
• Come let us sing of a wonderful love
• For all the love
• Jesu, Jesu, fill us with your love
• My song is love unknown
• O love that will not let me go
• Love is his word
• Let there be love
• Lord, the light of your love is shining
• For God so loved the world

- God is love, his the care
- My Lord, what love is this
- God is love, let heaven adore him
- God of love
- God's love is deeper
- I'm black, I'm white, I'm short, I'm tall

Introduction

How many of us, if travelling abroad, would attempt to speak the language of the country where we are staying? Some of us might give it a go if we're staying in France, Germany, Italy or Spain, perhaps having learnt at school the languages spoken there, or having heard a smattering of them over the years, but if we're travelling further afield – say to Russia, China, Nepal, Ghana, Peru or Greenland – we'll probably think twice before attempting to converse in the local lingo. Quite simply, we wouldn't know where to start, let alone how to finish! Language, in a sense, is a visible symbol of our divisions, the fragmented nature of our world, yet the ability to communicate does not rest solely on words. In the circumstances above we would be dependent on sign language to get our message across as best we can, proof indeed that actions sometimes speak louder than words, all of which takes us to the heart of this service. We are thinking today about the language of love; specifically, the way God's love is able to transcend the barriers that keep us apart. Through light-heartedly exploring some of the languages spoken in our world today we will move to consider the God whose love and purpose is able to speak to all.

Suggested readings

- John 3:16
- 1 Corinthians 13
- 1 John 4:7-21

Talk précis

What speaks all languages or, more exactly, is able to communicate across cultural, religious, political and racial boundaries? No, I'm not referring to a certain credit card, much though the advertisers might trumpet its claims! I'm speaking, of course, about love. And it is able to speak in such a way because it is finally beyond language, showing itself not just in words but also in deeds: a simple action, gesture, touch or embrace able to say and mean so much. Hardly surprising, then, that the good news of Christ has spoken to so many people in so many places across so many years, because at its heart it is, or at least should be, about God's free, total and unconditional love for all. This is the simple message of the gospel that has won the hearts of innumerable generations in innumerable parts of the world, and that takes us to the heart of the God we worship. God loved us before we ever knew him and will go on loving us for all eternity, nothing in heaven or earth able to stop him doing so. He loves us enough to have shared our humanity even to the point of death, offering his only Son for the life of the world. He loves us despite our faithlessness and disobedience, despite the ways we repeatedly let him down and stray from his side; like a good shepherd, he repeatedly seeks us out, patiently searching until he has restored us to his side. Quite simply, he *is* love, no other word so succinctly or accurately summing up his nature and purpose. That is the God we worship today, and that is the God who calls us to show love in turn, not through our own effort alone but through allowing his love to flow through us and from us, reaching out as an expression of worship and commitment in his name.

Have you grasped the extent of God's love for you? Have you understood how much he loves others? Have you recognised that helping to break down the barriers that separate us from God and one another involves being open to love working through you? God's love continues to reach out day after day. What about yours?

Prayers *Praise*
Almighty God,
    we praise you that your love extends to all,
    not limited to any time or place
    but extending to the ends of the earth
    and the same yesterday, today and tomorrow.
For your love that knows no bounds,
    Lord, we worship you.

We celebrate the love you have shown in Christ,
    his living, dying and rising not just for us
    but for all the world –
    every person,
    each individual,
    precious in your sight.
For your love that knows no bounds,
    Lord, we worship you.

We rejoice in that message of the gospel,
    able to speak across boundaries and barriers,
    whatever they might be,
    to win hearts,
    change minds
    and stir spirits,
    transforming innumerable lives over countless years.
For your love that knows no bounds,
    Lord, we worship you.

We exult in all your love means to us personally:
    the way it has challenged,

encouraged,
strengthened
and nourished,
helping us time and again to put the past behind us and start again.
For your love that knows no bounds,
Lord, we worship you.

We praise you for the knowledge that your love is constant;
that, however much we fail
and whatever we face,
you will never let us go.
For your love that knows no bounds,
Lord, we worship you.

Almighty God,
remind us afresh of your love for all,
and help us to love in turn,
so that we might show our worship not just in words
but also in deeds,
offered in the name of Christ
and for his kingdom.
Amen.

Thanksgiving
Lord Jesus Christ,
for the greatness of your love –
shown upon the cross,
shining in our lives,
reaching out into the world –
with joyful hearts
we thank you.

For the love we have shared –
with family and friends,
with fellow Christians
and with you –
with joyful hearts
we thank you.

For those who work to show your love in action –
ministering to those in need,
working for justice,
striving to break down barriers of prejudice, hatred and hostility –
with joyful hearts
we thank you.

For the power of love to transcend boundaries –
    building prejudices,
    healing rifts,
    cementing relationships –
    with joyful hearts
    we thank you.

Lord,
    we can never thank you enough for everything your love means
    and all it can accomplish,
    but we bring you our prayer,
    and with it our lives,
    seeking to express our gratitude through who we are
    and all we do,
    for your name's sake.
Amen.

Confession

Gracious God,
    we speak so easily of love and the unity it brings,
    yet so often our lives give out a different message.
For our part in all that divides and destroys,
    Lord, have mercy.

In our daily relationships,
    even with those closest to us,
    we can be selfish, cruel or thoughtless,
    acting or speaking in ways that wound,
    goad,
    demean,
    dishearten.
For our part in all that divides and destroys,
    Lord, have mercy.

In our attitudes, despite our best intentions,
    prejudice and partiality still lurk,
    preconceptions, assumptions and value judgements breeding fear,
    ambivalence,
    even hostility,
    preventing any meaningful dialogue or meeting of minds.
For our part in all that divides and destroys,
    Lord, have mercy.

Even within the Church we are all too often divided,
    not just between denominations
    but over theology, ethics and worship,
    what should be healthy diversity and mutual respect

all too easily translating into intolerance,
condemnation
and schism.
For our part in all that divides and destroys,
Lord, have mercy.

Forgive us, O God, for so much
that negates the love you would have us show
and undermines the message of the gospel.
Teach us that, whatever may divide,
far more unites us in Christ,
and help that truth to shape and shine through our lives,
to the glory of your name.
Amen.

Intercession
Sovereign God,
though your love seeks to unite,
we are conscious of so much that still divides,
wounding and scarring the lives of many.
Hear, then, our prayers for others.

In a world of inequality
we pray for the poor:
so many denied the essentials of life –
food and water,
shelter,
education and healthcare.
Provide the resources they need to build a better future,
and stir those like us who have plenty
not to be content to make token gestures of support
but to promote a fairer and more loving world.
Lord of all,
may your love bring hope, healing and harmony.

In a world of religious tension,
where faith so often polarises rather than unites,
inciting hatred,
persecution,
violence,
war,
we pray for dialogue,
respect
and reconciliation –
a willingness to see beyond differences to shared values and aspirations.
Lord of all,
may your love bring hope, healing and harmony.

In a world of racial inequality
    we pray for those who still face discrimination,
    rejection,
    hostility
    or abuse;
    their customs,
    convictions
    or simply the colour of their skin
    blinding people to the common humanity we share.
Break through the barriers of bigotry and ignorance,
    so that each may be accorded their true worth.
Lord of all,
    may your love bring hope, healing and harmony.

In a world of political instability
    we pray for societies, countries and continents divided from within,
    wrestling with factional in-fighting,
    sectarian conflict
    or civil war.
Grant the ability to look beyond ideology
    and to work for the common good
    in partnership with those of contrasting convictions.
Lord of all,
    may your love bring hope, healing and harmony.

In a world of conflict
    we pray for the Church,
    called to embody unity in Christ
    yet all too often divided itself.
Move through your Spirit to create openness to different traditions,
    diverse experiences,
    diverging emphases,
    so that variety might mean strength rather than weakness,
    openness to new ideas rather than entrenchment in old.
Lord of all,
    may your love bring hope, healing and harmony.

Sovereign God,
    tend your broken world
    and mend its divisions,
    through Jesus Christ our Lord.
Amen.

Closing prayer
Gracious God,
   send us on our way
   with the language of love shining from our eyes,
   spilling from our lips,
   and speaking in all we do and are.
Amen.

Order of Service

Integrate the foreign language/dialect phrases into both parts of the Talk within this service, asking people in each case to guess/translate what is being said.

- Key verse
- Introduction
- Hymn
- Prayer of praise
- Reading
- Talk (Part 1)
- Prayer of thanksgiving
- Hymn
- Music
- Reading
- Talk (Part 2)
- Prayer of confession
- Hymn
- Music
- Prayer of intercession
- Hymn
- Closing prayer

TASTE

11 Taste and see

A family service exploring our sense of taste

The aim of this service is to emphasise that, just as we do not know what food is like until we taste it, so we can only make up our minds about what it feels like to know and serve Christ by experiencing it for ourselves.

Key verse

Taste and see for yourselves that the Lord is good; happy are those who take shelter in him.
Psalm 34:8

Resources

You can use the idea for this service in a number of ways. You may wish to link worship to a meal, moving from the latter into a simple act of devotion using the prayers, readings and hymns below. Such a service might lead naturally into a celebration of the Lord's Supper. Alternatively, you might stage a family service, in which case you will need a wide variety of food items which young people (and other members of the congregation) can be invited to identify while blind-folded (either individually or as part of two teams). Either way, take care to ensure careful food hygiene standards at all times. Food-stuffs could include:

- Crisps, bread, biscuits, chocolate, jelly, sweets, fruit (various). As well as asking people what foodstuff they are tasting, you could see if they can distinguish between various brands of the same product.

Drinks could include:

- Milk, real fruit juices (various), cordials (various), fizzy pop (various), mineral water and tap water.

Suggested music

- 'Food, glorious food' from *Oliver!*
- 'Be our guest' from B*eauty and the Beast*
- A list of 500 songs about food can be found online at http://www.mixedup.com/foodsongs.htm.

Suggested hymns

- I hunger and I thirst
- I am the bread of life
- Guide me, O thou great Jehovah
- Bread of heaven, on thee we feed
- Faithful shepherd, feed me
- Who took fish and bread?
- Jesus the Lord said: 'I am the Bread'
- Here is bread

- Let us break bread together
- O Bread to pilgrims given
- Break thou the bread of life
- Bread is blessed and broken
- Here, Lord, we take the broken bread
- With this bread
- Bread of the world in mercy broken
- Be known to us in breaking of bread

Introduction

In our service today we focus on the gift of taste, first of all simply celebrating this often-overlooked sense before going on to explore what it might say metaphorically in relation to our experience of God. 'Taste and see that the Lord is good', urges the Psalmist, but what does that mean and how do we go about it? Through offering today a selection of foodstuffs for people to taste, we ask why tasting is so important, indeed irreplaceable, if we are to appreciate what food can offer. We ask similarly why tasting God's goodness for ourselves is equally vital if we are fully to understand what it means to love and know him, even as we are known and loved.

Suggested readings

- Psalm 34:1-10
- 1 Peter 2:1-10

Talk précis

How would you describe the taste of something to someone who has never come across it before: the taste of chocolate, for example, or coffee, honey, cheese, bread, milk, sausages, or potatoes? You could try using various adjectives – sweet, sour, bitter, bland and so forth – but while these might give some clue they would at best give the vaguest idea, never an appreciation of the real thing. The only way people can fully know what something tastes like is to taste it for themselves; the experience cannot be learned, borrowed or passed on by others, no matter how eloquent their description might be or sincere their efforts.

The same is true with understanding God: what it means to know and love him, to experience his presence in one's life, or to receive his comfort, guidance, blessings, strength, mercy and acceptance, peace and wholeness. Not, of course, that we can literally taste and see, but metaphorically we can do exactly that through committing our lives to his service, approaching him in praise and worship, trusting in his promises, and opening our hearts to the love of Christ and the living presence of the Holy Spirit. That requires an act of faith, a conscious decision on our part not so much to *taste* and see as to *test* and see. Do that, and we will indeed taste and know that the Lord is good.

Prayers   *Praise and thanksgiving*
Sovereign God,
    for all the ways we have tasted your love –
    reaching out to us before we knew you,
    accepting us as we are,
    enfolding us in your eternal embrace –
    with humble hearts
    we praise you.

For all the ways we have tasted your mercy –
    knowing ourselves forgiven,
    set back on our feet again,
    enabled to start again –
    with humble hearts
    we praise you.

For all the ways we have tasted your goodness –
    providing for our needs,
    enriching our lives with so many special things,
    granting us life now and the assurance of life to come –
    with humble hearts
    we praise you.

For all the ways we have tasted your power –
    strengthening and supporting us in times of need,
    guiding us through joy and sorrow, pleasure and pain,
    delivering us from evil –
    with humble hearts
    we praise you.

For all we have already tasted
    and all we have yet to taste –
    your love never exhausted,
    your mercy constant,
    your goodness brimming over
    and your power ever sure –
    with humble hearts
    we praise you.
Amen.

Confession
Gracious God,
    we *have* tasted that you are good,
    discovering that to be true in so many ways,
    but all too often and easily we have forgotten it.
Have mercy, O God,
    and help us to start again.

We have savoured your love,
   rejoicing in the knowledge that we matter to you,
   that you accept us as we are
   and care about our welfare,
   only then to forget all that when it matters most.
Have mercy, O God,
   and help us to start again.

We have celebrated your forgiveness,
   exulting in the knowledge that our mistakes are pardoned,
   the past done away with
   and the slate wiped clean,
   only then to sink back into feelings of guilt and failure.
Have mercy, O God,
   and help us to start again.

We have received your guidance,
   thanking you for answered prayer,
   for leading us through times of crisis
   and giving direction to our lives,
   only then to go our own way once again.
Have mercy, O God,
   and help us to start again.

We have experienced your power,
   praising you for overcoming obstacles,
   achieving things we never dreamt possible,
   giving us strength to face the demands of life,
   only then to think ourselves helpless in the face of adversity.
Have mercy, O God,
   and help us to start again.

We have recognised your presence –
   your hand upon us,
   your Spirit within,
   your nearness in Christ –
   only then to live without reference to you.
Have mercy, O God,
   and help us to start again.

Gracious God,
   help us to taste your goodness,
   today and every day,
   savouring afresh each moment all you have given
   and all you would have us enjoy.
In Christ's name we pray.
Amen.

Intercession
Living God,
 we have prayed for ourselves;
 hear now our prayer for others.

We pray for those who have not tasted your love,
 not having heard or responded to your call in Christ.
Help them to discover for themselves
 the joy of knowing and loving you.
In your mercy,
 Lord, hear us.

We pray for those who have tasted sorrow –
 the heartache of being rejected, deceived or betrayed;
 of watching a loved one suffer,
 or of enduring bereavement.
Grant that those who mourn will be comforted.
In your mercy,
 Lord, hear us.

We pray for those who have tasted suffering –
 the trauma of accident or injury,
 the unrelieved pain of chronic illness,
 the misery of life-threatening disease.
Grant strength and support,
 relief and release.
In your mercy,
 Lord, hear us.

We pray for those who have tasted need –
 not knowing where their next meal will come from,
 having nowhere to call their home
 and no way of supporting themselves or working for a better future.
Bring hope in their despair
 and grant them justice.
In your mercy,
 Lord, hear us.

We pray for those who have tasted hatred –
 victims of violence and terrorism,
 civilians in lands wracked by war,
 countries bitterly divided by race or religion.
Overcome all that keeps them apart,
 and grant reconciliation leading to lasting peace.
In your mercy,
 Lord, hear us.

Living God,
   hear these, and all our prayers,
   in Christ's name.
Amen.

Closing prayer
Loving God,
   create in us as we go on our way
   a hunger to know you better
   and a thirst to serve you more faithfully,
   so that we may taste more of your grace
   and our souls be filled with food that satisfies,
   through Jesus Christ.
Amen.

Order of Service

First order (including shared meal)
- Key verse
- Introduction
- Prayer of praise and thanksgiving
- Meal
- Prayer of confession
- Hymn
- Reading
- The Lord's Supper
- Prayer of intercession
- Hymn
- Closing prayer

Second order (family service)
- Introductory verses
- Introduction
- Hymn
- Prayer of praise and thanksgiving
- Reading
- Food tasting
- Hymn
- Food tasting
- Reading
- Talk
- Prayer of confession
- Hymn
- Prayer of intercession
- Hymn
- Closing prayer

TOUCH

12 A touching moment

A family service exploring our sense of touch

The aim of this service is threefold: first, to celebrate the gift of touch; second, to celebrate the touch of God's hand upon our lives; and third, to recognise the way in which we can touch the lives of others.

Key verse

Jesus reached out his hand and touched him.
Matthew 8:3a

Resources

A central part of the service is devoted to passing around various textured items (see below). Invite members of the congregation to close their eyes and, as each item is passed to them, to feel it for a few moments and reflect quietly on the gift of touch. How much do we take touch for granted? When did we last consciously reflect on the variety of textures around us? (Some may not warm to what they see as a 'touchy-feely' exercise, but don't be discouraged; it's impossible to please everyone all of the time!)

- Items with contrasting textures could include: felt, silk, cotton, wool, nylon, rubber, china, wood, leather, plastic, smooth glass, metal, cotton wool, a smooth stone, a leaf, Blu-Tack, writing paper, tissue paper, foam, bubble wrap, wax (small candle/tea light), a leaf, Plasticene, golf ball, sandpaper, jelly sweet, small piece of carpet, cork, pine cone, apple, conker, walnut, string.

Suggested hymns

- When I feel the touch
- Christ's is the world (A touching place)
- Father, I place into your hands
- Take my hands, Lord
- Put peace into each other's hands
- When the music fades

Introduction

Most of us like to think that we're 'in touch', whether we mean by that in touch with the times, with family and friends, with ourselves, with nature or with God. Yet touch is something we tend to be innately reserved about, especially, so people say, here in the UK. If two strangers inadvertently brush against each other in a crowded space, they will almost certainly automatically apologise. Indeed, even to talk about touch can seem vaguely licentious, prissy or new-age-like. Yet we have only to imagine being deprived of physical feeling to realise just how important this gift is to us and how much it contributes to our lives. As with all good things, it is worth celebrating for itself. For those who are Christians, it is also something to thank God for and to consider in terms of our relationship with him. Today, then, through touch we pause and ponder, worship and reflect, so that we might indeed be in touch with something deeper, above all with God, the giver of all.

Suggested readings
- Matthew 8:1-4
- Mark 5:21-43

Talk précis

Of all our senses the one we probably most take for granted is that of touch. The thought of losing one's sight or hearing fills most people with horror, and the idea of losing our sense of taste and smell is one we'd rather not think about, but the possibility of not feeling anything rarely occurs to us. Pause though to consider how special touch can be: the feel of freshly laundered sheets, a cat's fur, a baby's skin, silk or warm sunshine; or the reassuring feel of a pat on the back, hug or handshake – how much poorer our lives would be without such things.

On that level alone, touch is something to be celebrated, but to the Christian it speaks symbolically of something deeper. Just as Jesus reached out to touch the sick, the unclean and untouchables, ignoring social and religious taboos and so emphasising his love and acceptance of all, so we believe God continues to touch our lives today, not literally in the sense of a hand reaching down from heaven but deep within through the mysterious working of his Spirit: renewing, cleansing, healing, guiding, strengthening, instructing . . . and so we could go on. Unseen and often unrecognised, God reaches out to touch our hearts.

So, then, take away from today a deeper appreciation of the gift of touch, a greater awareness of the way this enriches our daily experience. But take away also the knowledge that God is able to touch each moment in a vital and wonderful way.

Prayers

Praise and thanksgiving
Caring and compassionate God,
    for all the ways you touch our lives,
    reaching out to bless,
    guide,
    heal
    and strengthen,
    in grateful praise
    we worship you.

For the touch of your hand in times of need –
    moments of fear and uncertainty,
    doubt and disbelief,
    crisis and challenge –
    in grateful praise
    we worship you.

For times you have lifted us up,
    setting us on our feet again,
    offering a shoulder to lean on,
    an arm to steady us
    and a hand to point the way,
    in grateful praise
    we worship you.

For the knowledge of your unfailing love,
    always there to encircle us,
    your arms outstretched to embrace
    and your hand ready to take hold,
    in grateful praise
    we worship you.

Caring and compassionate God,
    we place now our worship,
    our lives,
    our loved ones
    and our world
    into your hands, as,
    in grateful praise
    we worship you.
Amen.

Confession

Forgiving God,
    to our shame and sorrow we have resisted your hand,
    all too often shrugging you off,
    preferring our way to yours.
Reach out in mercy,
    and enfold us in your gracious love.

We have failed to recognise your touch,
    forgetful of your blessing,
    closed to your guidance,
    unaware of your presence.
Reach out in mercy,
    and enfold us in your gracious love.

We have kept others at arm's length,
    indifferent to need,
    oblivious to suffering,
    unwilling to get involved.
Reach out in mercy,
    and enfold us in your gracious love.

We have taken for granted the gift of touch –
   the comfort it can bring,
   reassurance offer,
   love express
   and solidarity articulate.
Reach out in mercy,
   and enfold us in your gracious love.

Open our hearts now to you,
   so that we may truly be in touch with you,
   one another,
   ourselves
   and all around us.
Reach out in mercy,
   and enfold us in your gracious love.

In Christ's name we pray.
Amen.

Intercession
Sovereign God,
   we pray for all who especially need your touch this day.
Encircle them now,
   embrace them always.

We think of the lonely –
   yearning for companionship:
   the knowledge that someone cares,
   the warmth of a human hand
   or the glimpse of a friendly face.
Encircle them now,
   embrace them always.

We think of the poor, the oppressed and the hungry –
   battling for survival,
   desperate for help,
   crying out for justice and compassion.
Encircle them now,
   embrace them always.

We think of the sick –
   those suffering in body and mind,
   seeking comfort,
   support,
   encouragement,
   understanding.
Encircle them now,
   embrace them always.

We think of the dying –
  wrestling with fear,
  enduring suffering,
  oppressed by sorrow.
Encircle them now,
  embrace them always.

We think of the bereaved –
  consumed by grief,
  numbed by shock,
  struggling with anger,
  crushed by helplessness.
Encircle them now,
  embrace them always.

Sovereign God,
  help us to reach out in love,
  expressing your care for all in whatever way we can.
Work in us and through us,
  so that our hands may be yours,
  and your touch be made known through our service.
Amen.

Closing prayer
Redeemer God,
  touch our lips,
  our hands
  and our feet,
  so that we might speak of you,
  work for you
  and walk with you.
Touch our hearts,
  our minds
  and our souls,
  so that we may fully love you,
  truly know you
  and wholly serve you.
Touch every moment of our lives in every part,
  sanctifying them by your grace,
  transforming them by your power
  and filling them with your love,
  through Jesus Christ our Lord.
Amen.

Order of Service

- Introductory verses: Matthew 8:3; 9:29; 14:36; 20:34; Mark 1:41; 6:56; Luke 5:13; 22:51
- Introduction
- Hymn
- Prayer of praise and thanksgiving
- Reading
- Tactile session (1)
- Hymn
- Tactile session (2)
- Talk
- Prayer of confession
- Hymn
- Prayer of intercession
- Hymn
- Closing Prayer

SCENT

13 Heaven scent

A service celebrating the world of scent

The aim of this service is to celebrate the gift of scent and to reflect on the biblical imagery of consecrating our lives as a fragrant offering to God.

Key verse

Strive then to imitate God, and live in love towards each other, just as Christ loved us and offered himself on our behalf, a fragrant offering and sacrifice to God.
Ephesians 5:2

Resources

If you want to stage this as a family service, then it is probably best to retain the scented items at the front of the church building and to invite children/people to come forward at a set point in the service to smell them. This way you can keep your eye on what is going on, particularly important if you are lighting candles, incense sticks and so on. You will probably need a few helpers to oversee proceedings. My own preference, however, is to make this a reflective service, in which case the various scented items can be passed around the church so that members of the congregation can quietly savour each one before passing it on. Candles, incense sticks, aromatherapy oils will, of course, need to be lit separately and not passed round. If these are used, it is probably best not to light them until near the end of the service in case asthmatic members of the congregation might suffer adverse effects (a warning to asthma sufferers could be given prior to and during the service).

Scented items could include the following:

- Fragrant flowers (at least one of these can be found in the garden or shops at almost every time of the year): hyacinth, jonquil, violet, lily-of-the-valley, bluebell, pink, rose, lavender, lily, jasmine, honey-suckle, tobacco plant (nicotiana)

- Aromatherapy oils

- Scented candles (strongly scented candles can be passed around unlit)

- Perfumes and aftershave lotions

- Incense sticks

Suggested hymns

- May the fragrance of Jesus fill this place
- May our worship be as fragrance (A living sacrifice)
- Worship the Lord in the beauty of holiness
- Brightest and best are the sons of the morning

Introduction Smell, so they say, is the most evocative of our senses. A scent caught on the breeze is able to kindle memories of moments long past in a way nothing else can quite begin to. How true that is I'm not sure, but there can be no denying how special a particular fragrance can seem. Our sense of smell, however, is not one we tend to give much thought to unless we lose it or are confronted by a fragrance that simply demands our attention. Then we realise how special it is. Not all scents, of course, are attractive or welcome, but today we focus on those that bring us pleasure, adding to the rich variety of the world God has given us.

Suggested readings
- Exodus 30:1-10
- Revelation 5:6-14

Talk précis What does our sense of smell have to do with God? Do scents, aromas, perfumes, fragrances really have anything relevant to say about faith and life? If you'd put that question to someone in Old Testament times, the answer would almost certainly have been yes. Conversation would swiftly have moved round to incense and the addition of fragrant oils to sacrifices, the idea being that the aroma was pleasing to God. Was this simply naïve anthropomorphism? In part perhaps, but it was also pragmatic, the smell of burnt offerings not exactly being appetising, to put it kindly, so anything to mask that had to be an improvement. But there was also a symbolic element to this practice, the odour of incense being likened to prayer and worship rising up to God. This idea is taken up in the book of Revelation, where the prayers of the saints are compared to incense ascending to heaven.

Does this symbolism do anything for you? It may do, it may not, but the point of this service is nothing so esoteric. It is simply to celebrate God's gift of scent and to thank him for the way it enhances our lives, whether it be through the fragrance of flowers, the appetising aroma of food cooking, the smell of freshly cut grass or other such evocative scents. These are part of the riches of God's creation, the vibrant tapestry of life, the beauty of the world around us; aspects of a gift to be savoured and celebrated, appreciated and acknowledged.

Prayers *Praise and thanksgiving*
Creator God,
    we celebrate today the scents that surround us –
    exotic,
    evocative,
    appetising,
    entrancing;
    a rich world of smell and fragrance;
    Lord, we praise and thank you.

For the aroma of freshly cooked bread,
   a meal cooking,
   herbs and spices;
   a rich world of smell and fragrance;
   Lord, we praise and thank you.

For the scent of perfume,
   potpourri
   and soap;
   a rich world of smell and fragrance;
   Lord, we praise and thank you.

For the smell of rain after a shower,
   the salty tang of the sea
   and the freshness of new-cut grass;
   a rich world of smell and fragrance;
   Lord, we praise and thank you.

For the bouquet of spring flowers,
   summer blooms,
   autumn leaves;
   a rich world of smell and fragrance;
   Lord, we praise and thank you.

For so much that evokes memories,
   sharpens our appetite,
   captures our imagination
   or soothes our spirit;
   a rich world of smell and fragrance;
   Lord, we praise and thank you.
Amen.

Confession
Gracious God,
   we yearn to bring our lives as a fragrant offering to you,
   but so often the reality falls short –
   our discipleship marred by dishonesty and disobedience,
   greed, pride and envy,
   thoughtless words and careless deeds,
   faults, failings and faithlessness.
Forgive us, Lord,
   and make us new.

We speak of honouring you,
   consecrating our lives in sacrificial service,
   but instead we live for self –
   our own pleasure,

own ends,
own aggrandisement.
Forgive us, Lord,
   and make us new.

We liken our prayers to incense rising up to you,
   its odour gladdening your heart,
   yet we all too rarely make proper time for you,
   more often than not scarcely giving you a second thought.
Forgive us, Lord,
   and make us new.

We talk of making a difference to the world we live in,
   bringing joy to others through our life and witness,
   our care and compassion,
   our love for all,
   but there is so little that truly sets us apart,
   that marks us out as your people.
Forgive us, Lord,
   and make us new.

Come among us
   and transform us by your grace,
   so that our lives might be imbued with the scent of your love
   reaching up to you in grateful praise
   and out to others in joyful service,
   through Jesus Christ our Lord.
Amen.

Intercession
Creator God,
   we have celebrated the beautiful scents that enrich our lives,
   but we pray now for those whose experiences are very different.

We think of the poor and hungry,
   surrounded by the scent of disease, deprivation and death,
   of polluted water and unsanitary housing,
   of failed crops and fields laid waste.
May your hand reach out to bless them,
   and the fragrance of your love pervade their lives.

We think of those who live with the scent of war,
   their lives blighted by conflict –
   the smell of blood and infected wounds,
   of gunfire and high explosives,
   of smouldering buildings, dust and debris.
May your hand reach out to bless them,
   and the fragrance of your love pervade their lives.

We pray for those in hospital waiting for surgery or other treatment –
reminded of their illness or impending operation
by the smell of disinfectant,
medicine
or anaesthetic.
May your hand reach out to bless them,
and the fragrance of your love pervade their lives.

We think of those who have lost their sense of smell,
no longer able to savour the everyday scents we take for granted –
to delight in the bouquet of flowers,
relish the aroma of food,
savour the smell of sea
or take pleasure in the odour of incense and perfume.
May your hand reach out to bless them,
and the fragrance of your love pervade their lives.

Gracious God,
reach out to these,
reach out to all,
and grant the sweet scent of your blessing,
through Jesus Christ our Lord.
Amen.

Closing Prayer
Loving God,
may the offering of our faith and worship
be as pleasing to you
as the fragrance of your goodness is pleasing to us.
Amen.

Order of Service

- Key verse
- Introduction
- Hymn
- Prayer of praise and thanksgiving
- Reading
- Distribution of scented items (1)
- Hymn
- Prayer of confession
- Reading
- Distribution of scented items (2)
- Hymn
- Talk
- Lighting of incense sticks and candles
- Prayer of intercession
- Hymn
- Closing prayer

Section Two
USING OUR IMAGINATION

MEDITATIONS

14 Worth pondering

A reflective service built around meditations

The aim of this service is to provoke reflection on the meaning and content of worship through meditations on the essential ingredients of worship, these taking the place of a talk or sermon. The meditations, introductions and prayers used have been taken from my books *To Put It Another Way*, *No Ordinary Man*, *Daily Prayer*, *Prayers for All Seasons* and *Are You Listening?* For ease of use, the prayers, introductions and meditations are set out in full within the suggested order of service.

Key verse   Grant that the words of my mouth and meditation of my heart might be pleasing to you, O Lord my rock and redeemer.
Psalm 19:14

Resources   The meditations needed for this service are set out in full in the suggested order of service. Other services could be held along the same lines, using either books of my own meditations or those of others. I list below a few suggestions:

- *No Ordinary Man* (books 1 and 2) –
  meditations on the ministry and message of Jesus
- *The Unfolding Story* –
  meditations on Old Testament stories and themes
- *To Put It Another Way* – meditations on the parables
- *Are You Listening?* – meditations on daily life
- *A Word for All Seasons* (Mary Hathaway)
- *Just Thinking* (Julian Hamilton)
- Eddie Askew (various publications)
- *Prayers of Life* (Michel Quoist)
- *Pilgrims Make Progress* (Howard Booth)

Suggested music   The hauntingly reflective music of Margaret Rizza would lend itself perfectly to a service of this kind. It could be used as an introit and at the close of worship, or interspersed with meditations. Recordings of Margaret's music include:

- *Fountain of Life*
- *River of Peace*
- *Fire of Love*
- *Chants and Songs*

Suggested hymns

For first hymn
- O praise ye the Lord
- I will sing your praises
- Praise to the Lord, the Almighty
- New every morning is the love
- All things praise thee, Lord most high.
- Give to our God immortal praise
- Praise, my soul, the King of heaven
- Praise the Lord, ye heavens, adore him

For second hymn
- Dear Lord and Father of mankind
- Forgive our sins as we forgive
- Have mercy on us, O Lord
- Lord, have mercy (from *The Source*)
- Lord, have mercy (Ghana; *Methodist Hymns Old and New*)
- Lord, have mercy (Russia; *Methodist Hymns Old and New*)
- There's a wideness in God's mercy

For third hymn
- Give thanks with a grateful heart
- Now thank we all our God
- Give to me, Lord, a thankful heart
- Thank you, Lord
- This thankful heart

For fourth hymn
- When I needed a neighbour
- Brother, sister, let me serve you (The servant song)
- Christ's is the world
- Make me a channel of your peace
- O Lord, all the world belongs to you
- God of the poor

Order of Service

Key verse

Introduction

'Think of it like this', we sometimes say when trying to help someone get their head round a concept or problem. In other words, try approaching it from a different angle, a new perspective, and see if things become any clearer. A fresh approach can cast an altogether different light on what is familiar, what we thought we had understood and even exhausted, throwing up all kinds of unexplored possibilities and unexpected dimensions. A reflective piece of writing or meditation can be one such tool, helping us to stand in another person's shoes or see things from a different point of view, and in worship that can add a new dimension to our reading and understanding of the Bible or our concept of the nature and call of God. Today we use reflective prayer and meditations to direct our thoughts. In place of a sermon we will hear reflections concerning praise, confession, thanksgiving, offering and intercession; reflections designed not to dictate rights and wrongs but to stimulate thought and lead us into worship of our own.

Hymn

Readings
Psalm 59:16-17 and Lamentations 3:22-24

Introduction to first meditation

It's always nice to receive praise, isn't it? Or is it? Actually, I think there are times when it is the last thing we want. When we've done something well, given of our very best, then praise is indeed welcome and we feel justifiably disappointed if it is withheld. If, though, someone offers it to us when we know it to be undeserved, then we feel patronised, embarrassed, even angry. As we rightly say, 'Praise where praise is due'.

With God there is never any question of that. We owe all we are to him, all that is and all that ever shall be. He is the giver of life now and of the life to come, the power behind the universe, the provider of all our needs – and so we could go on. So, likewise, with Christ – the one who gave his life for all, who brings hope and healing to a broken world, who represents the ultimate embodiment of love. Words cannot begin to tell of what we owe.

Neither God nor Jesus needs our praise, but they welcome it as an expression of our commitment, a token of our gratitude and a sign of our faith. We do not offer that praise because we have to, or because it is expected of us, but simply because it is appropriate, the natural response to everything we have received; the only response that will do.

First meditation (for two voices)

Lord, I woke up this morning,
    the sun streaming in at the window,
    birds singing in the garden,
    a gentle breeze whispering in the trees –
    and I wanted to sing for joy,
    to shout your praise from the rooftops,
    for suddenly life was wonderful,
    a taste of Eden.

I looked round,
   at the clouds scudding in the sky,
   children walking to school,
   bees buzzing among the flowers,
   and the dew glistening on the grass,
   and I wondered how I could ever fail to notice these,
   how my eyes could be blind and my soul closed
   to the loveliness of life.
Yet it happens, Lord, all too often.
I wake up and feel pressure rather than promise,
   a sense of burden rather than blessing.
I get dressed,
   go to work,
   talk to friends,
   walk in the park,
   but though my eyes see all, my soul sees nothing,
   thoughts turned inwards instead of out,
   on my own little world instead of the world beyond.
But this morning was different,
   for you opened my eyes to the miracle of life
   and the beauty within it,
   so I bring you now my praise,
   and offer this prayer:
   teach me to *see*, Lord, new every morning.

My child,
   it's good to hear you,
   to witness your joy and glimpse your delight.
And, believe me, there's nothing I'd like better
   than to answer your prayer,
   to give you always what you feel this moment.
Yet I can't give that promise,
   for I know through experience
   that what you see today you will miss tomorrow,
   and what speaks to you now may seem silent then.
It's not your fault,
   just the way of the world –
   your mind distracted by each day's passing cares.
Though the dawn will break and the sun still shine,
   though the birds will sing and the flowers still bloom,
   you may wake tomorrow and be blind to it all,
   unmoved by life's beauty,
   untouched by my presence.
But whether you see me, or whether you don't,
   whether morning brings joy, or fills you with dread,
   take heart, for I am with you,
   close by your side,
   from the dawn of the morning to the end of the day.

Silent reflection

Prayer of praise
Great and wonderful God,
    we join with the great company of your people
    on earth and in heaven,
    to celebrate your majesty,
    to marvel at your love
    and to rejoice in your goodness.
You are our God,
    and we praise you.

We acknowledge you as the Lord of heaven and earth,
    ruler of space and time,
    creator of all,
    sovereign over life and death.
You are our God,
    and we praise you.

We salute you as the beginning and end of all things,
    the one who is greater than we can ever begin to imagine,
    higher than our highest thoughts,
    beyond human expression.
You are our God,
    and we praise you.

We affirm you as all good,
    all loving,
    all gracious,
    all forgiving,
    and we bring you now our worship,
    our faith
    and our lives,
    offering them to you in grateful adoration.
You are our God,
    and we praise you.
Amen.

Readings
Romans 7:15, 21; Psalm 32:1-5

Introduction to second meditation
How often have you attempted to turn over a new leaf, only to fall
back into your old ways before you know it? How often have you
made a New Year's resolution, only to break it before the first day is
out? As the old saying has it, 'the spirit is willing but the flesh is weak'.
Try as we might, sometimes we just can't seem to help ourselves –

temptation is too strong to resist. And it's easy at such times to lose heart or succumb to feelings of guilt. Yet we should never despair, for God is far less critical of us than we are of ourselves. He's grieved by our mistakes, of course, but, unlike us, he is always ready to forgive and forget, always ready to wipe the slate clean and help us begin again.

Second meditation (for two voices)

Why did I do it, Lord?
Why did I let you down again?
After all those promises,
   all those resolutions,
   why is it I rush towards temptation
   like a moth attracted to a candle?
I cannot seem to help it.
Time and again I tell myself,
   'This time will be different! This time I will not fail!'
But when the moment comes it's the same old story –
   I resist for a moment,
   a token gesture,
   but in my heart I know it won't be long
   before the excuses win the day,
   and I give in yet again.
Why, Lord?
Why am I so weak and foolish,
   unable even to live up to my own expectations,
   let alone yours?
Lord, I'm ashamed,
   ashamed of what I do and who I am,
   of having to come once more asking for your forgiveness
   when I have no right to expect it.
Forgive me.

My child, don't lose heart.
You did let me down, yes,
   and of course I'm disappointed,
   but I understand.
I know what's going on deep inside you,
   and I realise you'd like to be different
   even if you never quite succeed.
Keep trying, always,
   no matter how many times you fail,
   or how often you feel like giving up –
   that's all I ask.
You'll still make mistakes,
   never be perfect,

probably go on letting me down until your dying day –
   I realise that.
But believe me, I won't be half as hard on you
   as you are on yourself.
I may be disappointed,
   but so long as you're truly sorry
   I'll always be ready to forgive,
   and always ready to start again.
It's when you're no longer ashamed,
   when you don't care any more,
   when your mistakes don't seem to matter –
   it's then that I'll really start to worry,
   and then perhaps you should start worrying too.

Silent reflection

Prayer of confession

Loving God,
   we find it so hard to acknowledge our faults
   and recognise our weaknesses.
We are reluctant to lose face,
   and unwilling to accept that we might need to change,
   perhaps even radically reorient our lives.
Have mercy,
   and redeem.

All too often, we go on pretending,
   running from the truth,
   adding one error to another
   and straying ever further from your side.
Have mercy,
   and redeem.

Remind us that such evasion offers no peace,
   no prospect of inner contentment.
Give us instead, then, wisdom and humility
   to admit our mistakes
   and square up to our failings,
   acknowledging them openly to you,
   so that we might find forgiveness,
   and, where possible, make amends.
Have mercy,
   and redeem.
In Christ's name we ask it.
Amen.

Assurance of forgiveness
Romans 7:24-25

Hymn

Readings
Psalm 100:4-5; Psalm 92:1-2, 4

Introduction to third meditation

It's surprising how much people will do for a simple 'thank you'. In almost all of us there is a craving for appreciation, the need to feel valued and worth something. A simple expression of gratitude can mean as much as any material inducement, spurring us to new efforts and greater heights. Yet sadly, where it matters, 'thank you' is all too rarely said. The multitude of little tasks done for us day by day, the gestures of service behind the scenes, the unsung contributions to our lives, more often than not pass unnoticed, unrecognised. And I suspect the same is true in our dealings with God. Our prayers tend to be long on 'please' and short on 'thank you'. We ask so much of God and make so many requests of him, but when our prayers are answered, how many times, I wonder, do we make a point of showing our appreciation?

Third meditation (for two voices)

Lord, I sent a card today.
Nothing out of the ordinary,
   just a simple thank-you note for a special gift.
There was no need to send it,
   for it wasn't expected,
   and I very nearly didn't, time, as always, being short.
But that present had meant something to me,
   touched my heart,
   and I wanted to show my appreciation,
   to make it plain it wasn't just taken for granted,
   but that I was truly grateful.
Yet it struck me, Lord,
   as I popped that card into the post-box,
   that while I'm good on the whole at saying thank you to others,
   I'm pretty hopeless when it comes to you.
I'd never considered it before,
   the thought simply not occurring to me,
   but suddenly I realised my prayers are all too often 'please'
   and all too rarely 'thank you'.
It's true, isn't it, Lord?
I'm always after something –
   another problem to solve,
   another request,
   another need,
   another desire –
   and I bring them to you without a second thought,

almost automatically,
confident you'll help.
But when the crisis is over,
your answer given,
it's all forgotten,
nothing more said until the next time.
There's no excuse, Lord, I know that –
so today, quite simply, I want to say thank you;
thank you, for everything.

My child,
thank *you*.
It's good to hear you,
for, believe me, you're not the only one
who fails to thank me.
I'm inundated each day by a multitude of people
with a multitude of requests,
a myriad of problems –
yet a modicum of gratitude.
'Do this', they tell me,
'Do that',
'Give me strength',
'Hear my prayer'.
And I do,
willingly,
only too glad to grant my blessing.
I don't demand a response or even expect one,
love bringing its own reward,
but to know I've touched a life and given joy
means as much to me as it would to anyone.
In fact there's only one thing more special,
and that's when someone not only says thank you
but shows they mean it –
responding when I offer guidance,
trusting when I offer strength,
risking when I offer freedom,
rejoicing when I offer life.
Do that, my child –
show gratitude in action –
and words no longer matter,
for it's all the thanks I need.

Silent reflection

Prayer
Loving God,
we have so much to thank you for,
so much that is good and special.

Day after day you bless us,
    week after week you answer our prayers,
    year after year you meet our needs.
We cannot thank you enough for your great goodness,
    yet the truth is we rarely thank you at all.
Forgive us for taking your gifts for granted,
    for letting familiarity blind us to how fortunate we are,
    and so failing to thank you for all you have given.
Forgive us for being swift to ask for your blessing,
    yet slow to acknowledge your generous response when you give it.
Teach us to receive your innumerable gifts with heartfelt gratitude,
    and to show our thanks not just in words
    but in our daily living –
    in lives that gratefully celebrate the wonder of your love.
Amen.

Reading
Luke 21:1-4

Introduction to fourth meditation
'And now the collection will be received.' It's surprising how often you hear announcements like that in church. Even more common is to hear members of the congregation use the same terminology. It may be innocent enough, but, personally, it makes me wince, for it can subconsciously encourage a fundamental misunderstanding of what Christian giving is all about. The implication is that we give out of duty: not because we may but because we must, because it is expected of us. What a contrast between that and the widow at the treasury. Humanly-speaking her gift was pathetic, barely worth the bother of counting it, but as far as God was concerned it was a priceless treasure, because it was given not as a collection but as an offering. She gave it because she wanted to, because she was eager to respond, and she gave sacrificially because she wanted to tell God how much he meant to her.

We can apply her example to the giving not only of our money but also of our time, our prayers, our love and our service. Do we truly *offer* those to God, or do we give them mechanically, half-heartedly, grudgingly? Do we bring them out of routine or habit, or as a spontaneous expression of love and thanksgiving? 'It's the thought that counts,' we are often told. In terms of our response to God, those are words well worth pondering.

Fourth meditation
I was ashamed, if I'm truthful,
    desperately praying that no one would notice me,
    for what would they think

when they saw those two miserable coins of mine;
what sort of person would they take me for?
They seemed little short of an insult,
worse, in some ways, than bringing nothing at all,
and, believe me, I'd toyed seriously
with staying away altogether to spare my blushes.
It had been different once,
when my husband was alive –
then I could hold my head up in any company,
my gifts, if not extravagant, more than generous.
But now, times were hard,
a matter of getting through from one day to the next as best I could;
life's little luxuries a thing of the past,
and many of its necessities too.
Yet there was one thing I was resolved to do, come what may,
even if it meant going short,
and that was to continue offering something to God.
So there I was, that day in the temple,
surreptitiously bringing my feeble gift.
It wasn't much, I know,
not in the eyes of the world, anyway,
but to me it was a small fortune,
the last thing I had in the world.
Well, you can imagine my horror when I arrived there
to find this crowd with Jesus watching.
It was my worst nightmare come true,
my pathetic offering exposed to the full glare of public scrutiny,
and I felt certain I would die of shame,
waiting with weary resignation
for the inevitable howl of laughter or snort of disgust.
And when Jesus nodded towards me
I could feel the colour rising to my cheeks,
skin crawling with embarrassment.
Yet then he spoke,
his words, would you believe, not of condemnation but praise,
singling me out as an example to follow
rather than object of ridicule.
It's the thought that counts, we sometimes say,
and Jesus understood how true that was.
He somehow knew how much that gift had cost me,
and to him those small pieces of copper were like nuggets of gold!
I went out that morning with my heart singing,
head held high after all,
and I brought my offering from then on
without any hesitation or any sense of unworthiness,
for I understood that God sees things differently than we do,

that he measures the gift not by how much it's worth,
but by how much it means!

Prayer
Gracious God,
    you give to us out of love,
    more and more blessings poured out upon us day after day.
Forgive us for so often giving to you out of habit or duty.
We make our offering in worship because it is expected of us.
We make time for personal devotion because we feel we ought to.
We make time for others because our conscience pricks us.
The result may seem worthy enough,
    but the true value is small.
Teach us instead to give joyfully,
    not because we must but because we may.
Teach us to offer our money,
    our worship
    and our service
    as a gesture of love
    and an expression of our appreciation.
Help us to understand that it is not the gift that matters
    so much as the spirit in which it is given,
    and may that awareness inspire the worship we offer to you,
    through Jesus Christ our Lord.
Amen.

Offering and blessing of gifts

Hymn

Reading
Matthew 25:31-46

Introduction to fifth meditation
Do you remember your first chemistry experiment at school? Almost
certainly it involved a piece of litmus paper, dipped into a test-tube
of liquid to see if it turned red or blue, indicating acid or alkali.
There is something of that test in the words of Jesus concerning the
sheep and the goats, only this time the test concerns something very
different – how faithfully we have responded to Christ.

What are the distinguishing features we should look for? Doctrinal
soundness? Faith that can move mountains? Gifts of the Spirit? An
impeccable record of church attendance? Not according to this par-
able, they're not. What counts, rather, is whether we have responded to
people in need; whether we have shown our faith in action, expressing

through our care and compassion the love of Christ. That, we are told, is the litmus test of Christian discipleship. Of course, we need to consider such words in the light of Christ's teaching concerning mercy and forgiveness, but we should not use that to evade or tone down their challenge. Faith may not depend on works but it ought to result in them, at least in part. The warning here is not so much that Jesus will reject us but that, through turning our back on others, we may find that *we* have rejected *him.*

Fifth meditation (of two Christians on the day of judgement)
(For two voices, alternately; second voice in italics)

I wasn't much of a Christian, the way I saw it.
(I wasn't a bad Christian, the way I saw it.)
Test me on doctrine and I'd be lost completely,
(Test me on doctrine and I'd have a ball,)
   the complexities of theology a mystery to me.
   (the niceties of theology a delight to me.)
My prayer life?
(My devotional life?)
That wasn't much better,
(That was spot on,)
   the words somehow never seeming to flow,
   (the words coming so easily,)
   discipline hard to achieve.
   (discipline coming naturally.)
It was the same with the Bible, I'm sorry to say;
(It was the same with the Bible, I'm glad to say;)
   I found most of it a closed book.
   (I knew it inside out.)
I tried hard enough, heaven knows,
(I hardly had to try,)
   but, let's face it, it's not the easiest of books to read,
   (for, let's be honest, it's such a wonderful book to read,)
   so many passages serving to puzzle rather than inspire.
   (every passage seeming to leap out and speak to me.)
And as for obedience, well, the less said about that the better,
(And as for obedience, well, I'm not one to boast,)
   for I kept slipping back into my old ways,
   (only it was as though my old self had died completely,)
   temptation catching me unawares,
   (temptation brushed aside,)
   my relationship with God a shadow of what it should have been.
   (my relationship with God everything it could be.)
So you can see what I mean, can't you? –
(So you get my point, don't you? –)

not much of a Christian, all told –
(*not a bad Christian, all told –*)
and as I stood there before Jesus, I feared the worst,
(*and as I stood there before Jesus, I had no fears whatsoever,*)
uncertain of his verdict, to say the least.
(*confident of his verdict, to put it mildly.*)
You can imagine my relief, can't you?
(*You can imagine my shock, can't you?*)
'Come, you that are blessed by my Father.'
(*'Depart from me . . . you that are accursed.'*)
I couldn't believe my ears!
(*I thought I was hearing things!*)
What had I done to deserve such blessing?
(*What had I done to deserve such punishment?*)
When had I ever put myself out for Jesus?
(*When had I ever let Jesus down?*)
Yet I had, time and again, without ever realising it.
(*Yet I had, day after day, without ever realising it.*)
When I reached out to the needy,
(*When I turned my back on the needy,*)
   when I responded to the poor,
   (*when I ignored the poor,*)
   when I visited the sick,
   (*when I recoiled from the sick,*)
   I was serving Jesus,
   (*I was failing Jesus,*)
   easing his pain,
   (*adding to his pain,*)
   expressing his love.
   (*denying his love.*)
I'm not much of a Christian, I still think that,
   (*I wasn't a bad Christian, I really believed that,*)
   yet, happily, I got one thing right –
   (*yet I got one thing hopelessly wrong –*)
   I responded to others,
   (*I put myself before others,*)
   I showed I cared,
   (*I didn't care,*)
   and now love brings its own reward.
   (*and now I must pay the price.*)
God moves in mysterious ways.
(*God have mercy on me, a sinner.*)

Silent reflection

Prayer of intercession

Loving God,
  we are reminded today that, in terms of this world's resources,
  we are the lucky ones –
  those with food in our belly
  and a roof over our head,
  with ample water and medicine,
  and with access to education, technology and so much else –
  our lives brimming over with good things.
Reach out to all denied the resources of life,
  and help us to reach out in turn.

Forgive us our complacency in the face of the world's evils
  and our share in an order
    that not only perpetuates the divide between rich and poor
    but also actively widens the gap.
Hear now our prayer for the millions less fortunate than us –
  those for whom hunger is a daily reality
  and for whom a lifetime of poverty
  is all that the future seems to offer.
Reach out to all denied the resources of life,
  and help us to reach out in turn.

Teach us to give sacrificially in response to their need
  and, more than that, to work for change,
    doing all in our power to help build a fairer world
    until that day when your kingdom dawns
    and all wrongs are righted.
Reach out to all denied the resources of life,
  and help us to reach out in turn.

In Christ's name we ask it.
Amen.

Hymn

Closing prayer

Eternal God,
  put your hand upon us,
  your arms around us,
  and your Spirit within us,
  so that we may recognise your presence,
  hear your voice,
  receive your guidance
  and grasp more of who and what you are,
  through Jesus Christ our Lord.
Amen.

DRAMA

15 Acts of worship

A reflective act of worship using sketches/drama

The aim of this service is to use drama/sketches/mime to bring home the message of the gospel. Drama is intended to speak for itself, so no suggestions for a talk are included.

Key verse

The key verse for this service will depend on what theme you choose for the sketches/drama.

Resources

- *Worship Interactive* (Michael Forster)
- *Sketches for the Church Year* (David Walker)
- *Conversations on the Way* (Tim Storey)
- *Parables Lite* (Mike Stone)
- *More Parables Lite* (Mike Stone)
- *After Goliath* (Janet Eastwood)
- *Living the Story* (Judith Rossall)
- *Buried Treasure* (Tony Bower)
- *Sketches with Scalpels* (Paul Herbert)
- *The Word in Action* (Michael Forster)

Suggested hymns

- Tell me the old, old story
- I will sing the wondrous story
- Proclaim, proclaim the story
- Timeless love! We sing the story
- God is working his purpose out
- Tell his praise in song and story
- We've a story to tell to the nations

Introduction

'Tell me the old, old story', begins the well-loved traditional hymn, and those words capture a vital truth at the heart of our faith. What we believe is not just a list of theoretical truths, a collection of abstract principles or a statement of certain beliefs about the ultimate nature of reality; it concerns rather a continuing story – the saga of God's creative purpose and dealing with humankind; the drama of the life, death and resurrection of Christ; the ongoing tale of the life of the Church and our own life stories. In this service through sketches and plays, each telling a story in themselves, we are invited to consider the wider backdrop of God's purpose into which our lives are woven, and to respond in worship and thanksgiving.

Suggested readings

Readings for this service will depend on the plays/sketches you choose and need to be tied in with these.

Prayers   *Praise and thanksgiving*
Sovereign God,
   we celebrate today your eternal purpose,
   shaping our world,
   our lives,
   our universe –
   giving form, meaning and direction to all you have made.
For your mighty acts,
   before,
   within
   and beyond all,
   joyfully we praise you.

We rejoice that we are not here by chance,
   thrown together into an impersonal and chaotic universe,
   our brief span of no consequence
   and all our striving,
   dreaming,
   hoping
   and believing
   an empty illusion.
We marvel that,
   on the contrary,
   each of us matters to you,
   our lives held in your hands,
   our well-being of infinite importance in your eyes,
   our names written in your book of life.
For your mighty acts,
   before,
   within
   and beyond all,
   joyfully we praise you.

We acknowledge that to you belong power and glory,
   honour and acclamation,
   for you are the creator of all,
   the one in whom we move and have our being,
   at work in our world,
   moulding history,
   fashioning the present
   and constantly rewriting the future,
   setting before us each moment the possibility of new beginnings,
   a fresh chapter,
   an unfolding story of faith.
For your mighty acts,

before,
within
and beyond all,
joyfully we praise you.

Receive, then, our worship,
and speak now, through all we share together,
of the continuing drama of salvation,
begun in Christ,
continued through his Spirit,
and awaiting final resolution in your fullness of time.
For your mighty acts,
before,
within
and beyond all,
joyfully we praise you.
Amen.

Confession
Gracious God,
too often we lose sight of your purpose.
We say,
'Your will be done,
your kingdom come,
on earth as it is in heaven',
but we rarely fully consider what that means
either for life now
or the life to come.
For the muddled saga of our lives
and the incomplete story of our faith,
merciful Lord, forgive us.

We wander aimlessly through life,
lurching from one whim,
one demand,
one goal,
one pursuit to another,
blown by the wind of fashion,
ambition,
self-interest
or passing fancy,
living only for the present moment
with little sense of a wider canvas.
For the muddled saga of our lives
and the incomplete story of our faith,
merciful Lord, forgive us.

We have been equally careless in our relationship with you,
    content to drift along in faith,
    grasping incidental details of your love
    rather than exploring the whole story –
    our understanding incomplete
    and our response inadequate.
For the muddled saga of our lives
    and the incomplete story of our faith,
    merciful Lord, forgive us.

Most foolish of all,
    we have deceived ourselves,
    pretending that all is well,
    imagining we understand all we need to know,
    believing we can control our own destiny
    and attempting to bend your will to our wishes.
Instead of responding to your word,
    the message of the gospel,
    we have substituted our own storyline,
    hopelessly muddling the plot.
For the muddled saga of our lives
    and the incomplete story of our faith,
    merciful Lord, forgive us.

Gracious God,
    have mercy.
Teach us not just to speak of your will
    but also actively to seek it,
    consecrating ourselves to your service
    and walking where you might lead,
    through Jesus Christ our Lord.
Amen.

Intercession
When the story of life is one of sorrow –
    marked by tragedy,
    betrayal,
    bereavement –
    Lord of all,
    write a fresh chapter of hope.

Where the story of life is one of suffering –
    marked by injury,
    disability,
    disease,
    Lord of all,
    write a fresh chapter of hope.

Where the story of life is one of injustice –
   marked by oppression,
   prejudice,
   exploitation –
   Lord of all,
   write a fresh chapter of hope.

Where the story of life is one of need –
   marked by poverty,
   hunger,
   homelessness –
   Lord of all,
   write a fresh chapter of hope.

Where the story of life is one of addiction –
   marked by drugs,
   alcohol
   or other dependency –
   Lord of all,
   write a fresh chapter of hope.

Where the story of life is one of hatred –
   marked by violence,
   terrorism,
   war –
   Lord of all,
   write a fresh chapter of hope.

Where the story of life is one of evil –
   marked by greed,
   corruption,
   crime –
   Lord of all,
   write a fresh chapter of hope.

Where the story of life is one of emptiness –
   marked by despair,
   emptiness,
   disillusionment –
   Lord of all,
   write a fresh chapter of hope.

Come among us, Lord –
   redeem,
   rewrite,
   refashion our world,

so that your love might triumph
and your gracious purpose be fulfilled,
through Jesus Christ our Lord.
Amen.

Closing prayer
Walk with us, O God,
and direct the course of our continuing story,
so that each day may be a new chapter,
each moment a fresh page,
rich in promise
and full of hope,
until that day when the threads are drawn together
and the mysteries of life are resolved in the light of your love
and the joy of your eternal kingdom,
through Jesus Christ our Lord.
Amen.

Order of Service

The aim of this service is to let sketches/drama do the talking, so a talk is not included.

- Key verse
- Introduction
- Hymn
- Prayer of praise and thanksgiving
- Reading
- Sketch/drama
- Silent reflection
- Hymn
- Sketch/drama
- Silent reflection
- Prayer of confession
- Hymn
- Sketch/drama
- Silent reflection
- Prayer of intercession
- Hymn
- Closing prayer

POETRY

16 Poetry in motion

A reflective act of worship using words of poetry

The aim of this service is to use poems old and new to speak of God and to stimulate reflection on the message of the gospel in relation to daily life. The poems should speak for themselves, so no talk suggestions are offered for this service.

Key verse

Open my lips, O Lord, and my mouth will declare your praise.
Psalm 51:15

Resources

The resources for this service are, self-evidently, poetry. I use the term in its broadest sense, to include reflective material such as the 'Desiderata' and 'Footprints' (see suggestions below). Appreciation of poetry is obviously subjective, what appeals to some leaving others cold, so try to include a balance of material, ranging from rhyming to blank verse, from classic poems to Patience Strong. As an alternative to choosing poems yourself, you might like to invite members of the congregation to choose their own favourite poetry (which need not be overtly religious). You might be bolder still, and ask people to write their own poems, though this could prove awkward if some compositions prove too weak to use! Below, as well as giving titles of books of poems/reflective material that you might find useful, I reproduce some non-copyright material that may prompt ideas.

- *An Anthology for the Church Year* (H. J. Richards)
- *The Electric Gospel* (Peter Dainty)
- *The Electric Bible* (Peter Dainty)
- *Beside Still Waters* (anthology published by Kevin Mayhew)
- *Footprints* (an audio collection read by Susan Sayers and Martin Shaw)

Desiderata
Go placidly amid the noise and the haste,
and remember what peace there may be in silence.
As far as possible without surrender be on good terms with all persons.
Speak your truth quietly and clearly;
and listen to others, even to the dull and the ignorant,
they too have their story.
Avoid loud and aggressive persons,
they are vexations to the spirit.

If you compare yourself with others,
you may become vain or bitter;
for always there will be greater and lesser persons than yourself.
Enjoy your achievements as well as your plans.
Keep interested in your own career, however humble;
it is a real possession in the changing fortunes of time.

Exercise caution in your business affairs,
for the world is full of trickery.
But let not this blind you to what virtue there is;
many persons strive for high ideals,
and everywhere life is full of heroism.
Be yourself. Especially do not feign affection.
Neither be cynical about love;
for in the face of all aridity and disenchantment
it is as perennial as the grass.
Take kindly the counsel of the years,
gracefully surrendering the things of youth.

Nurture strength of spirit to shield you in sudden misfortune.
But do not distress yourself with dark imaginings.
Many fears are born of fatigue and loneliness.
Beyond a wholesome discipline, be gentle with yourself.
You are a child of the universe,
no less than the trees and the stars;
you have a right to be here.
And whether or not it is clear to you,
no doubt the universe is unfolding as it should.

Therefore, be at peace with God, whatever you conceive Him to be.
And whatever your labours and aspirations in the noisy confusion of life,
keep peace in your soul.
With all its sham, drudgery and broken dreams,
it is still a beautiful world.
Be cheerful.
Strive to be happy.

Max Ehrmann, 1927

I asked . . .
I asked for strength that I might achieve;
I was made weak that I might learn humbly to obey.
I asked for health that I might do greater things;
I was given infirmity that I might do better things.
I asked for riches that I might be happy;
I was given poverty that I might be wise.
I asked for power that I might have the praise of men;
I was given weakness that I might feel my need of God.
I asked for all things that I might enjoy life;
I was given life that I might enjoy all things.
I received nothing that I had asked for;
but everything that I had hoped for.
Almost despite myself my unspoken prayers were answered;
I am, amongst all men, most richly blessed.
Amen.

I said to the man
I said to the man
who stood at the gate of the year,
'Give me a light that I may tread safely
into the unknown.'
And he replied,
'Go out into the darkness
and put your hand into the hand of God.
That shall be to you
better than light
and safer than a known way!'
So I went forth
and finding the Hand of God,
trod gladly into the night.
                    M. Louise Haskins (1875-1957)

From *Lines composed above Tintern Abbey*
To look on nature, not as in the hour
Of thoughtless youth; but hearing often-times
The still, sad music of humanity,
Nor harsh nor grating, though of ample power
To chasten and subdue. And I have felt
A presence that disturbs me with the joy
Of elevated thoughts; a sense sublime
Of something far more deeply interfused,
Whose dwelling is the light of setting suns,
And the round ocean and living air,
And the blue sky, and in the mind of man:
A motion and a spirit, that impels
All thinking things, all objects of all thought,
And rolls through all things. Therefore am I still
A lover of the meadows and the woods,
And mountains; and of all that we behold
From this green earth; of all the mighty world
Of eye, and ear – both what they half create,
And what perceive; well pleased to recognise
In nature and the language of the sense
The anchor of my purest thoughts, the nurse,
the guide, the guardian of my heart, and soul
of all my moral being.
                    William Wordsworth (1770-1850)

The tables turned
Up! up! my Friend, and quit your books;
Or surely you'll grow double:
Up! up! my Friend, and clear your looks;
Why all this toil and trouble?

The sun above the mountain's head,
A freshening lustre mellow
Through all the long green fields has spread,
His first sweet evening yellow.

Books! 'tis a dull and endless strife:
Come, hear the woodland linnet,
How sweet his music! on my life,
There's more of wisdom in it.

And hark! how blithe the throstle sings!
He, too, is no mean creature:
Come forth into the light of things,
Let Nature be your Teacher.

She has a world of ready wealth,
Our minds and hearts to bless –
Spontaneous wisdom breathed by health,
truth breathed by cheerfulness.

One impulse from a vernal wood
May teach you more of man,
Of moral evil and of good,
Than all the sages can.

Sweet is the lore which Nature brings;
Our meddling intellect
Mis-shapes the beauteous forms of things: –
We murder to dissect.
                    William Wordsworth (1770-1850)

The touch of the master's hand
'Twas battered and scarred, and the auctioneer
Thought it scarcely worth his while
To waste much time on the old violin,
But he held it up with a smile.
'What am I bidden, good folks?' he cried.
'Who will start bidding for me?'
'A dollar, a dollar' – then, 'Two!' 'Only two?'
'Two dollars, and who'll make it three?
Three dollars once, three dollars, twice;
Going for three' – But no,
From the room, far back, a grey-haired man
Came forward and picked up the bow;
Then wiping the dust from the old violin
And tightening the loosened strings,
He played a melody pure and sweet,
As sweet as a carolling angel sings.

The music ceased and the auctioneer,
With a voice that was quiet and low,
Said, 'What am I bidden for the old violin?'
And he held it up with the bow.
'A thousand dollars, and who'll make it two?
Two thousand! And who'll make it three?
Three thousand, once; three thousand, twice;
And going, and gone!' said he.
The people cheered, but some of them cried,
'We do not quite understand
What changed its worth?' Swift came the reply;
'The touch of the Master's hand.'

And many a man with life out of tune,
And battered and scarred with sin,
Is auctioned cheap to the thoughtless crowd,
Much like the old violin.
A 'mess of pottage', a glass of wine,
A game – and he travels on.
He's 'going' once, and 'going' twice,
He's 'going' and almost 'gone'.
But the Master comes, and the foolish crowd
Never can quite understand
The worth of a soul, and the change that's wrought
By the touch of the Master's hand.

Myra Brooks Welch

On another's sorrow
Can I see another's woe,
And not be in sorrow too?
Can I see another's grief,
And not seek for kind relief?

Can I see a falling tear,
And not feel my sorrows share?
Can a father see his child
Weep, nor be with sorrow fill'd?

Can a mother sit and hear,
An infant groan, an infant fear?
No, no! never can it be!
Never, never can it be!

And can He who smiles on all
Hear the wren with sorrows small,
Hear the small bird's grief and care,
Hear the woes that infants bear,

And not sit beside the nest,
Pouring pity in their breast;
And not sit in the cradle near,
Weeping tear on infant's tear;

And not sit both night and day,
Wiping all our tears away?
O, no! never can it be!
Never, never can it be!

He doth give His joy to all;
He becomes an infant small;
He becomes a man of woe;
He doth feel the sorrow too.

Think not thou canst sigh a sigh,
And thy Maker is not by;
Think not thou canst weep a tear,
And thy maker is not near.

O! He gives to us His joy
That our grief He may destroy;
Till our grief is fled and gone
He doth sit by us and moan.
                    William Blake (1757-1827)

The divine image
To Mercy, Pity, Peace and Love
All pray in their distress;
And to these virtues of delight
Return their thankfulness.

For Mercy, Pity, Peace, and Love
Is God, our Father dear,
And Mercy, Pity, Peace, and Love
Is Man, his child and care.

For Mercy has a human heart,
Pity a human face,
And Love, the human form divine,
And Peace, the human dress.

Then every man, of every clime,
That prays in his distress,
Prays to the human form divine,
Love, Mercy, Pity, Peace.

And all must love the human form,
In heathen, Turk, or Jew;
Where Mercy, Love, and Pity dwell
There God is dwelling too.
                    William Blake (1757-1827)

The road not taken
Two roads diverged in a yellow wood,
And sorry I could not travel both
And be one traveller, long I stood
And looked down one as far as I could
To where it bent in the undergrowth;

Then took the other, as just as fair,
And having perhaps the better claim,
Because it was grassy and wanted wear;
Though as for that the passing there
Had worn them really about the same,

And both that morning equally lay
In leaves no step had trodden black.
Oh, I kept the first for another day!
Yet knowing how way leads on to way,
I doubted if I should ever come back.

I shall be telling this with a sigh
Somewhere ages and ages hence:
Two roads diverged in a wood, and I –
I took the one less travelled by,
And that has made all the difference.
                    Robert Frost (1874-1963)

From *The Poetry of Robert Frost* edited by Edward Connery Lathem, published by
Jonathan Cape. Reprinted by permission of The Random House Group Ltd.

Death is nothing at all
Death is nothing at all.
I have only slipped away into the next room.
I am I, and you are you.
Whatever we were to each other, that we still are.
Call me by my old familiar name,
speak to me in the easy way you always used.
Wear no forced air of solemnity or sorrow.
Laugh as we always laughed at the little jokes we enjoyed together.
Play, smile, think of me.

Let my name be ever the household word that it always was.
Life means all that it ever meant.
There is absolutely unbroken continuity . . .
Why should I be out of mind because I am out of sight?

I am waiting for you . . .
for an interval . . .
somewhere near,
just around the corner.

All is well.
Henry Scott Holland (d. 1918)

Suggested hymns

No hymns relate directly to poetry so far as I am aware, but the majority of hymns are, essentially, poems – a point well worth bringing out during the service. Of the three hymns listed below, the first touches on the ability of words to move and inspire, while the other two touch tenuously on the theme of authorship.

- Your words to me are light and truth
- Author of faith, eternal word
- Author of life divine

Introduction

Words are curious things, aren't they? We can cram hundreds on to a page yet say virtually nothing; we can spend hours putting them together but succeed only in boring our listeners senseless; we can misuse them to wound, deceive, confuse and malign. Put them, though, in the hands of a poet and the merest few lines can captivate, comfort, challenge or inspire – in short, provide the essential ingredients of worship. Today, we use them for just that: to help express our praise and thanksgiving, to seek God's mercy, and to ask for his blessing on others. Through a selection of poems old and new, each in some way articulating the various poets' awareness and understanding of God, we seek to glimpse God for ourselves, to hear his voice, and to respond in worship and service.

Suggested readings

Two or three readings need to be chosen that fit with one or more of the poems you use in the service. For example the words of Romans 12:1-21 could be used to complement the thoughts of the Desiderata; or 1 Corinthians 15:12-23, 50-57 to reinforce the Henry Scott Holland reflection.

Prayers

Praise
Loving God,
    we recall today how you spoke your word and created the universe,
    awesome in scale,
    beyond anything our minds can fathom –
    a pointer to your own greatness,
    your infinite love,
    your sovereign purpose.
For your word of life,
    receive our praise.

We celebrate today that you spoke your word
   and brought this world into being,
   rich in life,
   wonderful in its beauty,
   filled with so much to fascinate,
   celebrate,
   inspire
   and amaze.
For your word of life,
   receive our praise.

We rejoice that you spoke through Christ,
   proclaiming your word of love,
   mercy,
   peace,
   wholeness;
   the promise of a fresh start,
   new hope,
   life in all its fullness.
For your word of life,
   receive our praise.

We recall how you have spoken across the years,
   your word calling,
   challenging,
   renewing,
   empowering across the centuries;
   overcoming evil,
   overturning empires,
   transforming human lives.
For your word of life,
   receive our praise.

We celebrate the way you speak to us –
   through the words of Scripture,
   the words of hymns, songs, prayers and poems,
   the words of others,
   and your still small voice within –
   bringing guidance,
   comfort,
   rebuke
   and assurance.
For your word of life,
   receive our praise.

In gratitude we come,
    knowing that you are not silent
    but always prompting,
    teaching,
    speaking,
    leading,
    if only we have ears to hear,
    eyes to see,
    and hearts to respond.
Speak, then, now, through this time of worship,
    so that we go on our way
    rejoicing in your love,
    and equipped to serve you better.
For your word of life,
    receive our praise.

In Christ's name we pray.
Amen.

Thanksgiving

Living God,
    we thank you for those gifted with words,
    those who can weave language in such a way
    that it articulates the very fabric of life,
    speaking of our deepest needs,
    our highest aspirations,
    our greatest loves,
    and acutest sorrows.
For all the ways you speak,
    receive our thanks.

We thank you for the ways words speak to us:
    the comfort they offer,
    hope revive,
    interest engender
    and truth impart.
For all the ways you speak,
    receive our thanks.

We thank you for ways we can use words:
    to encourage others,
    communicate needs,
    express emotions,
    convey gratitude,
    all this and so much more.
For all the ways you speak,
    receive our thanks.

We thank you for words that speak of you:
    opening our eyes to the wonder of life,
    our minds to the breadth of your purpose,
    our hearts to the inpouring of your love
    and our souls to the mystery of your purpose.
For all the ways you speak,
    receive our thanks.

As you have spoken in days gone by,
    so we know you will speak again.
In grateful praise, then,
    we bring you our worship.
For all the ways you speak,
    receive our thanks.
Amen.

Confession
Eternal God,
    so often when you speak
    we refuse to listen.
Time and again we have resisted your call.
Forgive us.

We close our ears to words that rebuke –
    that question our lifestyles,
    expose our faults,
    reveal our selfishness,
    uncover our pretensions.
Time and again we have resisted your call.
Forgive us.

We close our ears to words that challenge –
    that call us to costly giving,
    risk-taking love,
    sacrificial service,
    demanding discipleship.
Time and again we have resisted your call.
Forgive us.

We close our ears to words that stretch –
    that ask us to think about our faith,
    our relationships,
    our motives,
    our commitment.
Time and again we have resisted your call.
Forgive us.

We close our ears to words we do not understand –
    language reflecting different concepts,
    different cultures,
    different worldviews
    and different convictions to our own.
Time and again we have resisted your call.
Forgive us.

Eternal God,
    we close our ears to so much,
    and the tragedy is that, in doing so,
    we close our lives as well,
    not only to others
    but also to you.
Time and again we have resisted your call.
Forgive us.

Teach us to hear,
    to listen,
    to pause
    and to ponder,
    so that we may be open to what you might say,
    through whomever you choose to say it.
In Christ's name we pray.
Amen.

Intercession

Lord of all,
    we pray for those whose words touch the lives of many:
    journalists and reporters,
    politicians and broadcasters,
    novelists, teachers
    and countless other communicators in a host of fields –
    those whose words have the power to change attitudes,
    influence behaviour,
    mould ideas
    and interpret truth.
Give them an awareness of the responsibility that comes with privilege,
    and grant them wisdom and integrity in all their work.
By your grace, speak *to* them and *through* them,
    in the name of Christ.

We pray for those who are closed to your word
    or who struggle to hear it fully –
    those who reject any idea of you,
    those who seek faith but cannot find it,
    and those who have made a commitment to Christ

but who find themselves struggling to honour it.
Speak your word of love
   so that they might meet you,
   know you
   and serve you.
By your grace, speak *to* them and *through* them,
   in the name of Christ.

We pray for those who refuse to hear your voice through others –
   their hearts closed by religious intolerance,
   racial prejudice,
   cultural bigotry
   or other blinkered attitudes.
Break through the barriers that change their minds,
   and give a genuine openness to others,
   and to your presence within them.
By your grace, speak *to* them and *through* them,
   in the name of Christ.

We pray for those who seek to proclaim your word
   and to discern more clearly what you would say –
   clergy,
   theologians,
   youth leaders
   and Christian workers in their various callings,
   together with Christians everywhere yearning to know you better,
   so that they might work and live more effectively for you.
By your grace, speak *to* them and *through* them,
   in the name of Christ.

We pray for those for whom you can seem strangely silent and distant –
   the sick,
   poor,
   homeless,
   lonely,
   bereaved,
   maimed,
   weak
   and despairing –
   all who cry out to you for help
   yet seem to find no answer.
By your grace, speak *to* them and *through* them,
   in the name of Christ.

Lord of all,
   speak your word into our troubled world,
   your word of peace, mercy and love,

and may it bring wholeness and healing,
joy and justice,
renewal and respect,
light and life.
In the name of Christ we ask it.
Amen.

Closing prayer
Lord of life, direct our ways,
help us love you all our days.
Though our faith is flawed and frail,
though we all too often fail,
through the words and deeds we share
show the world how much you care.
Take our hearts, our hands, our feet –
reach out now to all we meet.
Teach us how to serve and when.
Guide our footsteps, Lord. Amen.

Order of Service

Ensure you leave times for silence after the reading of poems so that members of the congregation have time to reflect on and respond to what they have heard. Since the poems are designed to speak for themselves, no space is left for a talk.

- Key verse
- Introduction
- Prayer of praise
- Hymn
- Reading
- Poem
- Silent reflection
- Poem
- Silent reflection
- Poem
- Silent reflection
- Prayer of thanksgiving
- Hymn
- Poem
- Silent reflection
- Poem
- Silent reflection

- Poem
- Silent reflection
- Prayer of confession
- Hymn
- Poem
- Silent reflection
- Poem
- Silent reflection
- Poem
- Silent reflection
- Prayer of intercession
- Hymn
- Closing prayer

HUMOUR

H.P. 492
M.P. 512

17 A sense of humour

A celebration of the gift of laughter

The aim of this service is to celebrate humour as a gift of God.

Key verses

A merry heart makes for a cheerful countenance, but a morose disposition crushes the spirit. Every day in life is wretched for the downtrodden, yet those with a cheerful heart feast continually.
Proverbs 15:13, 15

Resources

- *Christian Crackers* – a selection of jokes, anecdotes
- *A Great Western* (Lucy Moore) – a Christian pantomime
- *Mr Bean* video
- *Vicar of Dibley*

Suggested music

- *Spread a little happiness* (Sting)
- *Happy Talk* (Captain Sensible)
- *When you're smiling . . . the whole world smiles with you*
- *The Laughing Policeman*

Suggested hymns

- Give me joy in my heart
- Shout for joy
- Shout for joy and sing
- Make a joyful noise, all ye people
- Shout, shout for joy
- Joy, joy, joy
- If you want joy, real joy
- Fill your hearts with joy and gladness
- There's a river of joy
- You shall go out with joy
- To conclude this service, you may like to sing my adaptation below of the hymn by Bunty Newport 'Think of a world without any flowers'

Think of a world without any laughter,
think of a life without any wit;
think of a day without any humour,
think of a sermon without any quips.
We thank you, Lord, for laughter, wit and humour,
we thank you, Lord, and praise your holy name.

Think of a world without any smiling,
think of a party without any fun;
think of a joke without any punchline,
think of a language without rhyme or pun.
We thank you, Lord, for smiling, fun and punchlines,
we thank you, Lord, and praise your holy name.

Think of a world without any comedy,
think of a circus without any clowns;
think of a court without any jester,
think of a home without merry sounds.
We thank you, Lord, for comics, clowns and jesters,
We thank you, Lord, and praise your holy name.

Think of a world where all must be serious,
think of a church were everyone's grim;
think of a life where laughter is frowned upon,
think of a faith where humour is sin.
We thank you, Lord, for all we have to cheer us,
we thank you, Lord, and praise your holy name.

Introduction   Like most good things, laughter can be abused and distorted. It can degenerate into silliness or sarcasm, mockery or teasing, these all too often leading to hurt rather than pleasure. There is nothing funny about laughing *at* someone; laughing *with* them, however, is a different matter. It can defuse a tense situation; overcome barriers of fear, suspicion, pride or hostility; engender a sense of well-being, or simply spread a little happiness into the daily routine. Understood thus, humour is one of God's special gifts, to be celebrated, shared and enjoyed. Today, then, we make time to laugh together, not just thanking God for humour but consecrating it to his service.

Meditation   'Don't make me laugh,' he said.
And I knew what he meant,
for I've said it often enough myself.
But today, Lord, I'm asking the opposite –
make me laugh, please,
for of all your gifts there is none more precious than laughter.
Not the laughter of mockery – I don't mean that –
    jeering at someone in their misfortune,
    but the ability to laugh *with* the world and *at* myself –
    to greet life with a smile,
    a wry grin,
    seeing the funny side of even the darkest moments;
    serious when I have to be,
    but recognising the foolish, the absurd and comical,
    and sharing the joke with you.
Teach me that, Lord;
    give me the wisdom,
    the confidence,
    the faith,
    and the humility I need,
    to look at the solemnity and the tragedy of life,
    and yet see the wonderful humour within it all.

My child,
    thank you for your prayer,
    for seeing me as I am
    rather than as I'm so often painted.
It gladdens my spirit to hear you,
    for all too many regard me as solemn and sombre,
    a tight-lipped, po-faced God,
    with never a smile or chuckle crossing my lips.
I understand why,
    for I can be stern,
    even forbidding,
    the issues I raise and the challenge I bring
    are no laughing matter.
And there are times when what passes as humour
    fills me with sadness –
    the cruel jibe,
    the sick joke,
    the heartless teasing,
    the cutting sarcasm.
But there's another side also,
    a part of me that revels in laughter
    and loves to see a smile on your faces,
    that delights in fun and longs to share it with you,
    for I know that happiness breeds happiness,
    and cheer spreads cheer,
    joy aids healing, and sunshine brings life.
So yes, there's a time to weep, but also to laugh,
    a time to mourn, but also to dance,
    and if you lose that balance,
    it's serious indeed,
    for I fear you've lost sight of me.

Suggested reading • Proverbs 15:13, 15; 17:22

Talk précis   Do Christians take themselves too seriously? And does the Church focus on the sombre and serious side of religion at the cost of a sense of fun? In the past the answer to such questions would almost certainly have had to be yes. For many outside the Church the idea of a stern and censorious Victorian clergyman reprimanding a congregation from the pulpit, or a puritan from Stuart times imposing a ban on dance, theatre and merry-making in general, just about epitomises their understanding of religion.

Today, thanks in part to TV series like *Father Ted* and *The Vicar of Dibley,* we have learnt to lighten up a little, recognising that poking fun at our foibles and eccentricities, the curious customs and peculiar practices within the Church, is not in any way the same as poking fun at God. On the contrary, laughter is God's gift, designed to uplift, comfort, forge friendships and enhance relationships. More than that, it can sometimes offer insights into truth far more effectively than a stern lecture or rebuke can ever begin to. Properly understood and sensitively employed, laughter does not belittle God or anyone else, but offers a more balanced perspective on all.

Prayers   *Praise and thanksgiving*
God of joy,
   we come to celebrate your great goodness –
   the happiness you give us now
   and the jubilation you promise for all eternity.
You turn tears into laughter,
   dismay into delight.
Gratefully we praise you.

We thank you for everything that brings a smile to our faces –
   that helps us see the funny side of life,
   humour that, even in times of sorrow,
   can uplift our spirits
   and cheer our hearts,
   bringing healing to body, mind and soul.
Gratefully we praise you.

We thank you for those with comic gifts –
   actors,
   writers,
   comedians,
   speakers –
   all those whose wit,
   levity,
   or sense of fun
   contributes to bringing a little light relief into our world.
Gratefully we praise you.

We thank you for the way humour enriches our lives,
   preventing us from taking ourselves too seriously,
   cementing relationships,
   defusing awkward moments
   and opening our minds to fresh perspectives.
Gratefully we praise you.

Accept, then, this time we bring you now,
    and through the amusement and merriment we share
    remind us of the joy you want us to experience,
    both now and for evermore.
Gratefully we praise you.
Amen.

Confession
Gracious God,
    with laughter,
    as with so much else,
    we can turn what is good into something evil,
    squandering and abusing a precious gift.
For misplaced, misguided humour,
    Lord, forgive us.

We have laughed *at* people rather than *with* them,
    poking fun,
    making jokes at their expense,
    our laughter belittling,
    mocking,
    wounding.
For misplaced, misguided humour,
    Lord, forgive us.

We have laughed at that which cheapens and degrades –
    at sick jokes,
    jibes,
    smut
    and sarcasm.
For misplaced, misguided humour,
    Lord, forgive us.

We have laughed at the wrong moment –
    when we needed to be serious,
    when we needed to share the sorrow of others,
    when we needed to pause and take stock
    rather than shrug something off with a smile.
For misplaced, misguided humour,
    Lord, forgive us.

Gracious God,
    teach us when to laugh and when to weep,
    when to smile and when to be serious,
    when humour is right and when it is out of place.
Teach us to use your gift wisely,
    in the name of Christ.
Amen.

Intercession
Sovereign God,
    alongside laughter we know that life brings tears,
    alongside joy, its share of sorrow,
    and we are conscious that for some people pain outweighs pleasure,
    suffering precludes celebration,
    and heartbreak obscures happiness.
Lord of love,
    we bring them to you in prayer.

We pray for those for whom simply surviving is a deadly serious business:
    the countless people in our world who strive merely to feed,
    clothe
    and house themselves,
    each day a battle against hunger, thirst and disease,
    life ravaged by warfare, injustice or natural disaster.
Lord of love,
    we bring them to you in prayer.

We pray for those whose hearts are heavy:
    victims of broken relationships and broken homes,
    those who have lost their jobs, their homes,
    their hopes, their livelihoods,
    those who mourn loved ones,
    those coming to terms with injury, disfigurement or terminal disease,
    those in the grip of depression and despair.
Lord of love,
    we bring them to you in prayer.

Sovereign God,
    in a world of so much good but so much evil,
    so much humour but so much heartache,
    smile upon us
    and bring laughter to the eyes and hearts of all.
Amen.

Closing prayer
Go now,
    with laughter in your eyes,
    a smile on your lips,
    a song in your heart,
    and merriment in your soul,
    and share the joy that Christ has given you.
Amen.

Order of Service

- Introductory verses: Job 8:21, Psalm 126:1-3; Ecclesiastes 3:4; Luke 6:21; Philippians 4:4
- Introduction
- Hymn
- Prayer of praise and thanksgiving
- Humour slot
- Sketch/tape/video
- Humour slot
- Hymn
- Prayer of confession
- Humour slot
- Sketch/tape/video
- Humour slot
- Meditation: 'Don't make me laugh,' he said
- Hymn
- Reading: Proverbs 15:13, 15; 17:22
- Talk
- Hymn
- Humour slot
- Sketch/tape/video
- Humour slot
- Prayer of intercession
- Hymn
- Closing prayer

Section Three
USING OUR GIFTS

FLOWER-ARRANGING

18   Say it with flowers

A floral service celebrating the beauty of plants and flowers

The aim of this service is to celebrate the gift of flowers and to worship God through them.

Key verses

See how the wild flowers grow, pay heed to them. They do not labour or weave, yet I can assure you that not even Solomon in all his grandeur was decked out like one of these.
Matthew 6:28b-29

Resources

- The resource for this service, naturally enough, is a variety of floral displays. Flowers do not come cheaply, of course, unless you are lucky enough to have a congregation of skilled and generous gardeners. Almost certainly you will need to buy in a fair proportion, so it is worth incorporating this service into a bigger event (i.e. a flower festival) lasting two or three days. Ensure as wide publicity for this as possible, advertising the service as the climax of the event. It may be that you can persuade local flower-arranging groups to share in the event, perhaps with the cost of flowers being shared. Alternatively, this might be staged as an ecumenical service, using the flower-arranging skills from all the churches in your neighbourhood.
- You might also wish to display posters, pictures and banners around the church building, but ensure that these do not detract from or clash with the floral displays. A headline banner or poster at the front of the sanctuary (perhaps used as the theme for the event) could display the following quotation: 'Flowers are God's thoughts of beauty taking form to gladden mortal gaze' (Anonymous).

Suggested music

- *Roses from the south* (Johann Strauss)
- *Tulips from Amsterdam*
- *The last rose of summer* (Irish folk song)
- *Edelweiss* (from *The Sound of Music*)
- *Where have all the flowers gone?* (Pete Seeger)

Suggested hymns

- For the beauty of the earth
- Jesus is Lord! Creation's voice proclaims it
- All creatures of our God and King
- Lord, you created a world full of splendour
- When God made the garden of creation
- There's a song in the heart of creation
- At the dawning of creation
- Creation sings!

- Creator of the starry height!
- Father, Lord of all creation
- Think of a world without any flowers
- Lord of creation (chant)

Introduction

'Say it with flowers', the slogan says, and few sales pitches could have been more successful in rooting themselves in the public consciousness. We send flowers to express condolences at a funeral or share joy in a wedding; to say sorry or thank you, to express congratulations or ease disappointment; to let someone know we love them or that we're thinking of them at a difficult time. Flowers, quite simply, speak all kinds of languages, and today we will be using them to speak one more: to talk to us of God. That, of course, is nothing new; from earliest times people have looked at flowers and been moved by their simple beauty to postulate a creative hand behind them, a sovereign being by whose purpose such loveliness has come into being. Today we take that idea further, using not only flowers themselves but also the gifts of those who arrange them to speak of God's creative power and his love for all. Take time, then, as you look around you now and more closely during the service, simply to take in the colour, fragrance, wonder and beauty that surrounds us, celebrating and giving thanks to God for it all.

Suggested readings

- Isaiah 35:1-2
- Isaiah 40:6-8
- Matthew 6:25-34

Talk précis

'See how the wild flowers grow, pay heed to them. They do not labour or weave, yet I can assure you that not even Solomon in all his grandeur was decked out like one of these' (Matthew 6:28b-29). What was Jesus saying here – that we can prove the existence of God through something as simple as a flower? Of course not. Though a flower's beauty does indeed speak of God to the eye of faith, to others it is a cause to celebrate but nothing more. No doubt Jesus would have celebrated that beauty as much as anyone, and no doubt too he saw God's hand behind the natural world, but as with so much of his teaching he uses it here to point to deeper truths still – truths concerning God and his love for all. 'If God clothes the flowers of the field like this,' he says, 'which though here today will be tossed on a bonfire tomorrow – then how much more richly will he clothe you, O you of little faith?' (Matthew 6:30). The analogy has a twin message. On the one hand, it brings an assurance of God's care and provision, calling us to recognise that if he pays such attention to detail over even the smallest flower, then *how much more so* must that be true for us. On the other hand, Jesus obliquely reminds us here that even the most long-lasting flowers are short-lived, a display such as the one around us past its best in a couple of weeks at most. And in a sense the same is true of human life: our span may be longer but our health and beauty fade too as the years pass. As the prophet Isaiah so starkly put it, 'All people are like grass, as short-lived as the flowers of the field. The grass shrivels and the flower fades when God breathes upon them; surely people are like grass' (Isaiah 40:6b-7). Yet, of course, that is not the end of the story, because for Isaiah, as for Jesus, this comparison offers a reminder of how much God loves us and how much more richly he longs to bless us. 'The grass shrivels and the flower fades, but the word of our God will stand for ever' (Isaiah 40:8) – a word that, through Jesus, brings the promise of life beyond death, a glory that will not fade, blessing for all eternity. 'See how the wild flowers grow, pay heed to them.' See the flowers displayed around us. Who would have thought they could say so much?

Prayers   *Praise and thanksgiving*
Maker of all,
    we praise you today
    for the wonder of plants, trees, bushes and flowers
    and the way they so wonderfully enhance and enrich our lives.

For the simple beauty of a snowdrop,
    the elegance of a lily,
    the lushness of a lawn
    and the grandeur of an oak,
    Creator God,
    receive our thanks and joyful worship.

For the fragrance of a rose,
    the perfume of jasmine,
    the scent of violets
    and the bouquet of lavender,
    Creator God,
    receive our thanks and joyful worship.

For carpets of bluebells,
    fields of poppies,
    drifts of daffodils
    and banks of primroses,
    Creator God,
    receive our thanks and joyful worship.

For fronds of ferns,
    bark of trees,
    leaves of bushes
    and blades of grass,
    Creator God,
    receive our thanks and joyful worship.

For cottage gardens,
   herbaceous borders,
   formal bedding
   and arboretums,
   Creator God,
   receive our thanks and joyful worship.

For those who breed plants,
   propagate them,
   cultivate
   or arrange them,
   Creator God,
   receive our thanks and joyful worship.

For the flowers that surround us now,
   so rich in colour,
   so varied in scent,
   so simple yet speaking so profoundly of you,
   Creator God,
   receive our thanks and joyful worship.

In the name of Christ we pray.
Amen.

Confession
Gracious God,
   you remind us in the words of Isaiah
   that the grass withers
   and the flowers fade,
   and we are conscious that what is true of this life
   can be equally true of our discipleship.
For our fragile faith
   and fleeting commitment,
   Lord, have mercy.

Time and again we resolve to serve you better,
   to make more time for prayer and devotion,
   to conquer our weaknesses,
   to be more loving in our words and deeds,
   but time and again that resolve is short-lived,
   our good intentions soon forgotten,
   the new leaf we thought we'd turned over left shrivelled and dying.
For our fragile faith
   and fleeting commitment,
   Lord, have mercy.

We have lost the sparkle that once marked our discipleship,
   the first flush of enthusiasm,
   trust,
   vision
   and devotion that characterised our early years
   having grown faded and jaded.
For our fragile faith
   and fleeting commitment,
   Lord, have mercy.

We have lost our sense of wonder in your presence,
   taking for granted your goodness,
   becoming over-familiar with your grace
   and complacent concerning your purpose.
For our fragile faith
   and fleeting commitment,
   Lord, have mercy.

Gracious God,
   renew our faith,
   restore our trust
   and revive our vision,
   so that the love we profess today
   and the service we offer
   may be as vibrant and real the next day
   and every day,
   through Jesus Christ our Lord.
Amen.

Intercession
Creator God,
   surrounded by so much beauty,
   we are reminded today of the delicate balance of nature
   and the need to steward it wisely,
   and so we pray for those entrusted with nurturing,
   protecting
   and preserving the natural world around us.
In all they do and decide,
   grant them wisdom, Lord.

We pray for conservationists, ecological groups and environmentalists –
   those who work,
   campaign,
   protest
   and petition
   to safeguard sites of special interest and natural beauty,
   or endangered species and habitats.

In all they do and decide,
    grant them wisdom, Lord.

We pray for town and county councils,
    parliament and the government,
    international leaders and environmental fora –
    all who must weigh up economic and ecological considerations,
    their decisions shaping not just the life of constituents and nations
    but potentially the very fabric of life itself.
In all they do and decide,
    grant them wisdom, Lord.

We pray for farmers and landowners,
    planners and developers,
    industry and multinational corporations,
    economic agencies and business leaders –
    those with a stake in harvesting this world's resources
    but also dependent finally on stewarding them responsibly
    to ensure not just sustainable growth but a sustainable planet.
In all they do and decide,
    grant them wisdom, Lord.

We pray for those developing recycling initiatives,
    locally, nationally and internationally –
    all who work to make possible reductions in waste,
    re-using materials,
    cutting pollution
    and saving energy.
In all they do and decide,
    grant them wisdom, Lord.

We pray finally for people the world over,
    and especially those like us
    who enjoy affluence compared to the many.
Inspire a sense of awareness,
    responsibility
    and concern,
    coupled with a resolve to help make a difference,
    however insignificant it might seem.
In all they do and decide,
    grant them wisdom, Lord.

In Christ's name we pray.
Amen.

Closing prayer
Almighty God,
   nurture the seeds of faith you have sown within us,
   so that trust, love, commitment and compassion
   might blossom within us,
   to the glory of your name.
Amen.

**Order of
Service**

- Introductory verses: Genesis 1:11-12
- Introduction
- Hymn
- Reading: Isaiah 35:1-2
- Prayer of praise and thanksgiving
- Hymn
- Viewing of flower display
- Hymn
- Reading: Matthew 6:25-34
- Talk
- Prayer of confession
- Hymn
- Prayer of intercession
- Reading: Isaiah 40:6-8
- Hymn
- Closing prayer

CRAFTWORK

19 Many gifts – one Lord

A service using banners, needlecraft, artwork and other forms of craftwork

The aim of this service is to recognise the artistic and creative gifts of individuals within the church fellowship, to thank God for them and to explore what they have to tell us about God and the Church as a whole.

Key verse

Worthy are you, Lord God, to receive glory, acclamation and sovereignty, for you created the earth and all that is in it; everything has been made by you, its existence down to your will.
Revelation 4:11

Resources

- For this service you will need as many craft, art, needlecraft, etc., exhibits as possible, so you need to plan and publicise the service well in advance. Put up notices several months beforehand inviting people, should they wish, to prepare something for the service; reinforce this with personal invitations to those you know to be particularly gifted. Compile a list of people who have committed themselves to make something so that you know there will be plenty to display on the day. Exhibits need not necessarily be on a religious theme, but it would be good to display them for a time afterwards; those that fit in with the church ambience will naturally lend themselves towards this – for example, banners for display, church kneelers/seat covers.

Suggested music

No music especially suggests itself for this service.

Suggested hymns

- Come to us, creative Spirit
- Creator Spirit, by whose aid
- Lord, you created a world full of splendour
- This is the day
- God our Creator
- I am a new creation
- This world you have made
- When God made the garden of creation
- God who made the earth

Introduction

'There is one body,' said the Apostle Paul, writing to the Corinthians and the Romans, 'but many gifts', and he proceeds to mention just a few. The list, though, is not for a moment intended to be exhaustive, and among those people he fails to mention are those specially gifted with their hands. The gifts they exhibit can come in a multitude of forms, some practical, others aesthetic, but all in their way add to the rich tapestry of life – painting, drawing, needlecraft, banner-making, carpentry, and metalwork to name but some – each an expression of the human creative urge, but to the eye of faith each in turn pointing also to the creative hand of God, the source, author and designer of life itself. Today, we celebrate the human creativity within our fellowship, and as we do so we celebrate also *God's* gifts in all their diversity, his awesome power that fashioned our universe, making possible everything we see displayed before us.

Suggested readings

- Genesis 1:1-31
- Isaiah 45:5-19
- Romans 12:1-8
- 1 Corinthians 12:4-11

Talk précis

Those gifted with their hands can make complex tasks look surprisingly easy. A cartoonist can create a lifelike caricature with a few strokes of a pencil; an interior decorator can plaster a wall or hang wallpaper in the time it takes most of us to prepare the materials; a carpenter can create a piece of furniture while we're still wondering where to start; and so we could continue. It's only when we attempt some of these creative tasks ourselves that we realise how difficult they are, and learn to appreciate the skill of those able to undertake them successfully.

Sadly, such gifts don't get a mention from the Apostle Paul when he writes of spiritual gifts in his letters to the Romans and Corinthians. In the first he writes of prophecy, ministry, teaching, giving, generosity, leading and showing compassion; in the second he speaks of wisdom, knowledge, faith, gifts of healing, miracles, prophecy (again), and speaking in tongues. All of these have their place, but the lists were never intended to be exhaustive, Paul writing about them largely because they were being abused. In every church, every fellowship, numerous gifts pass unsung, unnoticed, yet they are no less vital to our health as the body of Christ. That alone provides reason enough for this service, but there is a deeper lesson we can draw from the exhibits around us, for their creativity is a microcosm of the Creator of all, the handiwork of God in creation. As we celebrate together what human hands have made, let us celebrate also what God has made: the wonder of the world, the immensity of the universe, the miracle of life, the beauty and fascination of so much around us – and, above all, let us celebrate the new creation he is constantly effecting in our lives, forever taking what is and, like a potter moulding the clay, shaping what shall be.

Prayers

Praise

✗ Creator God
   we praise you for all you have fashioned with your hands:
   the universe in all its vastness,
   the earth in all its beauty,

the sea,
the sky,
hills,
mountains,
rivers,
streams –
all this, and so much more.
Maker of all that is,
has been
and shall be,
reverently we worship you.

We praise you for creating us,
bringing us into being as a potter moulding clay,
granting us life in all its fullness,
the ability to move,
feel,
think,
hear,
see
and infinitely more besides.
Maker of all that is,
has been
and shall be,
reverently we worship you.

We praise you that you are constantly at work,
striving to perfect your creation,
to overcome all that frustrates your will
or denies your love.
Maker of all that is,
has been
and shall be,
reverently we worship you.

We praise you for all you are able to do in our lives –
the way you take and use us in ways beyond our expecting,
transforming,
renewing,
equipping,
enabling,
making of each of us a new creation in Christ.
Maker of all that is,
has been
and shall be,
reverently we worship you.

Order of Service

- Introductory verses: Psalm 100:3; 136:5; 139:14; Isaiah 40:26; 41:20; 42:5; Ephesians 5:9; Colossians 1:16; Revelation 4:11
- Introduction
- Hymn
- Procession of banners and other craftwork
- Reading: Psalm 8:1-9
- Prayer of praise
- Hymn
- Viewing of craftwork
- Reading: Romans 12:3-8
- Hymn
- Talk
- Prayer of confession
- Hymn
- Prayer of thanksgiving and intercession
- Hymn
- Closing prayer

MUSIC

20 Make a joyful noise

A celebration of worship through songs and music

The aim of this service is to worship God through music and song.

Key verses
Be filled with the Holy Spirit and sing psalms, hymns and spiritual songs together, singing and making music to the Lord in your hearts. *Ephesians 5:18b-19*

Resources
- The principal resource for this service is the musical talent you have within your church fellowship. Ideally, the service should comprise a mixture of solo/duet/ensemble items and congregational singing. For the solo/duet/ensemble items you could simply ask for volunteers, but this may, of course, result in excruciating and potentially embarrassing offerings. If what matters most to you and the congregation is sincerity rather than musical quality, then no problem; otherwise you may prefer to vet participants and select those whom you know to be capable of a reasonable rendition. Whichever approach you adopt, remember that this is not intended to be a concert or musical talent show. It is probably best, therefore, for pieces played or sung to have some kind of religious theme or association.
- You may need some kind of hi-fi system to provide musical backing for singers. Ensure that the reproduction is of sufficient quality to be heard without distortion at the back of the church building.
- Ensure that there is a microphone/microphones for singers/musicians. Check in a prior rehearsal that there is no feedback from the amplification system, and arrange for someone who knows what she/he is doing to keep an eye on things during the service and to adjust sound levels as and when necessary.
- If musicians/singers require piano/organ/guitar accompaniment, make sure that this has been arranged and that the accompanist has been given the chance to prepare in advance.

Suggested music
- Music for this service is provided by members of the congregation, but *On wings of song* (Mendelssohn) could be an appropriate introduction to worship and a recording of *Thank you for the music* (Abba) would make a fitting ending to the service as people disperse after the closing prayer/blessing.

Suggested hymns
- For the music of creation
- When, in our music, God is glorified
- Father God, I wonder
- Jesus put this song into our hearts
- Lift up your voice

- When the music fades
- Come, let us join our cheerful songs
- Make a joyful noise, all ye people
- Shout for joy and sing
- Born in song!
- I will sing your praises

Introduction

Of all the ways of responding to God, few surely are more natural, universal or long-established than music or song. 'Sing a new song to the Lord,' say the Psalms; 'Make a joyful noise to the Lord'; and the Apostle Paul urges us to sing and make melody in our hearts. When we are happy or thankful we want to sing about it, to give vent to our joy; when we are in love our heart sings within us; whereas, for others, songs have expressed hardship, hope, sorrow, protest and so on – in short, the whole gamut of human experience. Today we come, as countless others have come before us, to make music to the Lord – through shared song and hymns, and through musical items sung or played for us, to lift up our hearts and voices, to offer our praise and express our thanksgiving, and to commit ourselves afresh to the service of Christ. Together, let us worship God.

Suggested readings

- Psalm 98:1-9
- Ephesians 5:15-20

See also *Order of Service*

Talk précis

Why are we here today? The obvious answer is to enjoy a good sing and a good tune, but, true though that might be, it's not the whole story. Yes, music and song are well worth celebrating for themselves, few things able to raise our spirits or express our feelings so well, but to play a meaningful part in worship there needs to be something more; namely that one simple but vital ingredient pinpointed by the Apostle Paul in his letter to the Ephesians. 'Sing psalms, hymns and spiritual songs,' he writes, 'singing and making music *to the Lord in your hearts*' (Ephesians 5:18b-19). There's the key, the thing that makes this time together more than a sing-song, concert or celebration of music. Everything we share today is offered *to the Lord,* and for that to be so it needs to come *from the heart,* articulating what we feel deep within, speaking of our love and commitment, our thanks and praise, our sorrow at our weakness and our desire to start again. Not just today then, but whenever you worship, don't just enjoy music but offer it from the heart to God, as a sign of your love, an expression of your commitment, an inegral part of your worship.

Prayers

Praise
Almighty God,
     we are here to make a joyful noise –
     to lift up our voices,

in an expression of worship
and an outpouring of adulation.
With choirs of angels and the great company of your people,
we join together in praise.

We are here to make melody in our hearts –
to declare your greatness,
celebrate your love
and rejoice in your grace.
With choirs of angels and the great company of your people,
we join together in praise.

We are here to offer songs of adoration –
to extol your name,
acknowledge your blessings
and proclaim your faithfulness.
With choirs of angels and the great company of your people,
we join together in praise.

We are here to sing hymns of acclamation –
to remind ourselves afresh of your awesome power,
your sovereign purpose
and your unfailing mercy.
With choirs of angels and the great company of your people,
we join together in praise.

Almighty God,
receive all we bring you now,
for we offer it gladly and reverently,
in the name of Christ.
Amen.

Thanksgiving
Living God,
we thank you for the gift of music –
for the joy of making it
and the delight of hearing it.
You have put a song of thanksgiving in our hearts,
and filled us with gladness.

We thank you for the way a song or tune can uplift our spirits,
capture our imagination,
or move us to tears.
You have put a song of thanksgiving in our hearts,
and filled us with gladness.

We thank you for the pleasure music gives to so many –
    the fun it brings,
    wonder evokes
    and happiness fosters.
You have put a song of thanksgiving in our hearts,
    and filled us with gladness.

We thank you for the gifts of composers and writers –
    their talent,
    sensitivity,
    and dedication.
You have put a song of thanksgiving in our hearts,
    and filled us with gladness.

We thank you for musicians –
    the time they put into learning,
    practising
    and performing.
You have put a song of thanksgiving in our hearts,
    and filled us with gladness.

Living God,
    we know that without music we would be so much the poorer,
    our world stripped of something special,
    our lives denied a precious gift,
    so today, through this time we share,
    we bring you our heartfelt thanks.
You have put a song of thanksgiving in our hearts,
    and filled us with gladness.
Amen.

Confession
Gracious God,
    our hearts should sing out for joy,
    for you have showered us with love
    and blessed us beyond measure,
    but so often we sing to a different tune.
For forgetting your love,
    Lord, have mercy.

We brood over our problems
    and fret about the future,
    forgetting that, whatever may come,
    you will support and strengthen,
    sufficient for all our needs.
For forgetting your love,
    Lord, have mercy.

We envy others,
    coveting what we do not have,
    our thoughts fixed on earthly gain
    rather than spiritual fulfilment.
For forgetting your love,
    Lord, have mercy.

We fritter away your many gifts,
    taking them for granted,
    exploiting them with no thought of tomorrow,
    or too preoccupied with other concerns to appreciate them fully.
For forgetting your love,
    Lord, have mercy.

We deny ourselves the joy of your presence,
    neglecting time for prayer and worship,
    ignoring your word,
    wandering from your side.
For forgetting your love,
    Lord, have mercy.

Gracious God,
    forgive us our foolish ways,
    and teach us to celebrate all you have given
    and all you will yet give,
    through Jesus Christ our Lord.
Amen.

Intercession

Lord of all,
    hear our prayer for those whose song is one of sorrow.

We remember those broken in body –
    overcome by sickness or disease,
    emaciated through starvation,
    maimed or injured through accident or acts of violence.
Uphold and uplift them,
    restore hope and joy.

We pray for those broken in mind –
    those oppressed by depression and despair,
    victims of Alzheimer's
    and those who are mentally disturbed or disabled.
Uphold and uplift them,
    restore hope and joy.

We think of those broken in spirit –
   their confidence crushed by failure and rejection,
   their trust in others and the future broken by betrayal,
   their faith in you destroyed by tragedy.
Uphold and uplift them,
   restore hope and joy.

In Christ's name we pray.
Amen.

Closing prayer
In the bustle of life
   as much as in worship,
   in the routine and mundane
   as much as moments set aside,
   may our hearts still sing within us,
   our spirits soar
   and our lives be filled with melodies of praise,
   through Jesus Christ our Lord.
Amen.

Order of Service

The number of solo items/duets, etc., you want to include will, of course, depend on the talent within your church fellowship. Try to ensure, however, a balance between individual and congregational items, so that everyone can both listen and participate.

- Introductory verses: Psalm 59:16; 66:2; 89:1; 92:1-2; 95:1-3; 101:1; 104:33
- Introduction
- Hymn
- Prayer of praise
- Scripture verses: Isaiah 5:1; Romans 15:9
- Musical item
- Congregational singing
- Musical item
- Scripture verses: 1 Corinthians 14:15; James 5:13
- Prayer of thanksgiving
- Hymn
- Reading
- Musical item
- Congregational singing

- Musical item
- Prayer of confession
- Hymn
- Reading: Ephesians 5:15-20
- Talk
- Hymn
- Musical item
- Congregational singing
- Musical item
- Prayer of intercession
- Hymn
- Closing prayer

DANCE

21 Lord of the dance

An expression of worship using the medium of dance

This service aims, through the medium of Christian dance, to express joy in worship and a celebration of discipleship.

Key verses

You have transformed my weeping into dancing; having removed my sackcloth, you have clothed me instead with joy such that my spirit cannot keep quiet for praise. Lord God, I will thank you to the end of time.
Psalm 30:11-12

Resources

- The principal resource you will need for this service is a dance troupe specialising in Christian dance. Unless you are lucky enough to have such a group in your church, there will, of course, be travelling expenses to meet, and possibly a fee as well. If you do not have such a group locally, then it may be that members within your fellowship may be willing to prepare a routine, but for this to be effective it will need careful practice and preparation.

- You may wish to involve younger children in this service, preparing a simple (or even encouraging spontaneous) dance for use during the service. If so, this will be enhanced by providing a selection of ribbons, sashes, etc., for the children to wave.

- An efficient hi-fi/amplification system to play backing music during the dance routines.

Suggested music

The choice of music to accompany dance routines must be left with the dancers themselves, except in the case of young children. The following pieces are suitable for children's participation, or could be played (either by the organist/music group or using recorded music) before and after the service, and during any interludes, such as the taking up of an offering, etc.

- 'Anitra's Dance' from *Peer Gynt Suite* (Grieg)
- 'Dance of the Sugar Plum Fairy' from *The Nutcracker* (Tchaikovsky)
- *Bolero* (Ravel)
- 'Dance of the Blessed Spirits' from *Orpheus* (Gluck)
- *Slavonic Dance* (Dvořák)
- 'Dance of the Little Swans' from *Swan Lake* (Tchaikovsky)
- 'The Swan' from *Carnival of the Animals* (Saint-Saëns)
- 'Dance of the Flutes' from *The Nutcracker* (Tchaikovsky)
- 'I could have danced all night' from *My Fair Lady*
- *Let's dance* (David Bowie)
- *Dancing queen* (Abba)

Suggested hymns

- I danced in the morning (Lord of the dance)
- Dance and sing
- Dance in your spirit
- O come and join the dance
- Let the mountains dance and sing
- Teach me to dance
- Sing a song of celebration (We will dance)
- I will dance, I will sing
- Where there once was only hurt (Mourning into dancing)
- Jesus Christ is waiting

Introduction

When did you last dance a jig of delight? For many of us the answer is probably never, for dance is one of those things people respond to in different ways. Some love it, some hate it. Some find it deeply moving while others are left completely cold, and though for some dance is a natural and spontaneous expression of their feelings, for others it would be forced and utterly unnatural. Yet the reservations of some should not deny dance its rightful place within patterns of worship, for it has a pedigree stretching back in history, to the time of David and the Psalms, and beyond. For David and many others, the joy they felt at God's goodness and blessing could not fail to put a spring in their step, setting them leaping and twirling for delight. Not that many of us, if any, would feel comfortable with a free-for-all – a waltz up the aisle, a conga round the church, a rumba in the pulpit or a jive in the vestibule – but thoughtfully planned and sensitively performed, or characterised by the spontaneous sincerity of children, it can speak *to* us and *for* us in a way beyond words.

Whether or not you are a natural dancer, open your heart now to the God who seeks always to see our spirit leap for joy within us as we celebrate the constancy of his love.

Suggested readings

It may well be that certain readings naturally complement the dance routines chosen for the service. The following passages, however, speak more generally about dance as an expression of worship:

- 2 Samuel 6:16-23
- Psalm 149:1-3
- Psalm 150
- Ecclesiastes 3:4

Talk précis

'There is a time to grieve,' says the book of Ecclesiastes (3:4), 'and a time to dance.' Some might feel that the time for the latter is not in worship, and if they mean by that a spontaneous dancing in the aisles, then they're probably right. It might find a place in some traditions but for most of us it just would not feel right. But, of course, those words of Ecclesiastes use dance in its widest sense, essentially as a metaphor for showing feelings of joy, jubilation, happiness, thanksgiving. It is the same virtually wherever dance is referred to in Scripture, the idea behind it being a spontaneous demonstration of gratitude and gladness, praise and delight; an outpouring of worship that cannot be contained. How we show such worship will depend on our temperament and character. Just as some *love* to dance and others hate it, as some naturally show their feelings while others are less demonstrative, so there are numerous kinds of worship – some formal, others free, some exuberant, others restrained. What matters is not the outside but the inside; whether we are open to express ourselves not just with our minds but also with our hearts; whether our soul can still dance within us, leaping for joy, exulting in God's goodness. The gift of dance, like all gifts, is given to some rather than all; the gift of a dancing spirit is for everyone.

Prayers

Praise and thanksgiving
Mighty God,
　　we have so much to celebrate,
　　so much to thank you for,
　　so much in our lives that is good and special.
Our heart leaps to you in gratitude,
　　our spirit dances in praise.

You have given a world full of beauty,
　　able to captivate,
　　intrigue,
　　excite
　　and inspire –
　　its riches constantly able to surprise us,
　　moving us to a sense of wonder and thanksgiving.
Our heart leaps to you in gratitude,
　　our spirit dances in praise.

You have given us families and friends,
　　the joy of human companionship:
　　the blessing of working together,
　　talking together,
　　laughing together,
　　being together.
Our heart leaps to you in gratitude,
　　our spirit dances in praise.

You have given us strength in times of weakness,
　　comfort in times of sorrow,
　　guidance in times of confusion,
　　hope in times of despair –
　　your love constantly surrounding us,
　　encouraging,

enfolding,
enabling.
Our heart leaps to you in gratitude,
   our spirit dances in praise.

You are with us now
   and will be with us always,
   nothing in life or death finally able to come between us,
   for your sovereign purpose
   and gracious love
   is stronger than anything that might fight against it.
Our heart leaps to you in gratitude,
   our spirit dances in praise.

Mighty God,
   hear our prayer
   and receive our worship,
   for we offer all to you in the name of Christ.
Amen.

Confession
Merciful God,
   though you have blessed us so freely,
   and though we speak of gladly responding,
   we all too rarely do so in practice.
For joyless faith
   and gloomy discipleship,
   Lord, forgive us.

We have brooded over problems, pressures and responsibilities,
   forgetting that you will give us strength to face them.
For joyless faith
   and gloomy discipleship,
   Lord, forgive us.

We have dwelt on what we do not have,
   allowing greed, envy and resentment
   to obscure all we have received.
For joyless faith
   and gloomy discipleship,
   Lord, forgive us.

We have been oppressed by guilt, weakness and failure,
   forgetting that in Christ you set us free
   and offer new beginnings.
For joyless faith
   and gloomy discipleship,
   Lord, forgive us.

We have focused on negatives rather than positives,
seeing faith in terms of what we *can't* do
instead of what we *can*;
as a set of rules and regulations
rather than an invitation to joyful living.
For joyless faith
and gloomy discipleship,
Lord, forgive us.

We have grown over-familiar with the gospel,
no longer reminding ourselves of its message,
no longer applying it to daily life,
no longer making the time for you we should.
For joyless faith
and gloomy discipleship,
Lord, forgive us.

Merciful God,
put laughter in our eyes,
delight in our hearts,
a skip in our step,
a smile on our lips
and a sparkle in our faith,
so that all we are and do
may testify to the joy we have found in you,
through Jesus Christ our Lord.
Amen.

Intercession
Lord of all,
hear our prayer for those in sorrow or need,
those whose lives are overshadowed by sickness,
tragedy,
worry
or want.
Turn their mourning to dancing,
their sackcloth to clothes of joy.

We think of those who are unwell:
those known to us,
those in hospital waiting for surgery
and those with permanent illness or disability.
Especially we pray for . . .
Turn their mourning to dancing,
their sackcloth to clothes of joy.

We think of those who are sad:
    those for whom life has brought disappointment,
    those hurt in relationships
    and those who have lost or face losing loved ones.
Especially we pray for . . .
Turn their mourning to dancing,
    their sackcloth to clothes of joy.

We think of those who are troubled:
    worried about family and friends,
    fearful of the future,
    consumed by anxiety and insecurity.
Especially we pray for . . .
Turn their mourning to dancing,
    their sackcloth to clothes of joy.

We think of those enduring hardship,
    victims of famine,
    disaster,
    oppression
    or war.
Especially we pray for . . .
Turn their mourning to dancing,
    their sackcloth to clothes of joy.

Lord of all,
    reach out into our bruised and bleeding world,
    and touch the lives of all who are broken or breaking.
May the light of your love shine through,
    bringing healing where there is disease,
    delight where there is dismay,
    peace where there is distress
    and hope where there is despair.
Turn their mourning to dancing,
    their sackcloth to clothes of joy.

In Christ's name we pray.
Amen.

Closing prayer
Lord of the dance,
    send us out with a spring in our step,
    a melody in our heart,
    and a spirit that leaps for joy.
May we match our steps to yours
    and follow where you might lead,
    this day and always.
Amen.

Order of Service

The service could open and/or close with a short dance procession/tableau.

- Introductory verses: Ecclesiastes 3:1, 4; Jeremiah 31:4b; Psalm 30:11-12
- Introduction
- Hymn
- Prayer of praise and thanksgiving
- Dance
- Reading
- Dance
- Hymn
- Reading
- Talk
- Prayer of confession
- Hymn
- Dance
- Prayer of intercession
- Hymn
- Closing prayer

Section Four
USING OUR MINDS

PROVERBS

22 Words of wisdom

A service exploring proverbs and sayings from the Bible and elsewhere

The aim of this service is to hear words of wisdom from the Bible or passed down across generations, and to reflect on what these might say to us today.

Key verses

Let those who are wise hear more and increase in learning; let those with insight acquire skill in understanding proverbs and sayings, the teachings of the wise and their conundrums. Fearing God is where knowledge begins; the foolish loathe wisdom and instruction.
Proverbs 1:5-7

Resources

- Print off well-known proverbs and sayings and display these round the walls of the church.
- Prepare some other proverbs/sayings, either printed or on a Power-Point/OHP presentation, leaving out a few key words (or perhaps the beginning/end of the proverb). Use the incomplete proverbs/sayings as a quiz during the service, asking if anyone can supply the missing words.
- For this service, you will also need a selection of proverbs and sayings on various themes, to be read, slowly and clearly, by readers chosen and prepared before the service. I suggest ten themes, proverbs for which are listed below:

On love
- Love looks not with the eyes, but with the heart. (William Shakespeare)
- We are shaped and fashioned by what we love. (Goethe)
- One pardons to the degree that one loves. (La Rochefoucauld)
- Love is the reward of love. (Schiller)
- He who falls in love with himself will have no rivals. (Anonymous)
- If love be timid, it is not true. (Spanish proverb)
- Love your enemies, for they tell you your faults. (Franklin)
- Love is not love when it asks for a reward. (W. R. Inge)
- Have Christians subconsciously retranslated the famous text, 'God so loved the world', into God so hated the world that he gave his only Son, that whoever does not believe in him should perish'? (Author unknown)
- Tell me, what is love?
  It is grief, anxiety, tears, and loss.

Why then do you love?
Because love is joy, certainty, laughter, gain.
(Frederic Vanson)

- Faith, hope and love endure, and the greatest of these is love. (1 Corinthians 13:13)
- A simple meal eaten where there is love is infinitely better than a feast soured by hatred. (Proverbs 15:17)

On hope

- Whoever wants to enjoy the glory of the sunrise must live through the night. (Anonymous)
- When the sun sets, the moon rises; when the moon sets, the sun rises. (Chinese proverb)
- A good hope is better than a bad possession. (Anonymous)
- The darkest hour is that before the dawn. (Anonymous)
- The bee sucks honey out of the bitterest flowers. (Anonymous)
- The tide never goes out so far but it always comes in again. (Anonymous)
- In the land of hope there is never any winter. (Anonymous)
- God comes at last when we think he is farthest off. (Anonymous)
- The future belongs to those who know how to wait. (Russian proverb)
- The optimist says we live in the best of all possible worlds. The pessimist is afraid that this may be true. (Anonymous)
- Unfulfilled hope brings sickness of heart, but when it is realised it is like a tree of life. (Proverbs 13:12)
- Suffering generates staying power, which in turn strengthens character, which in turn again yields hope; a hope that never lets us down, because God through his Holy Spirit has poured love into our hearts. (Romans 5:3b-5)

On truth

- Truth needs not the ornament of many words. (Anonymous)
- Truth may be blamed but cannot be shamed. (Anonymous)
- Truth is not only violated by falsehood; it may be equally outraged by silence. (Henri Frédéric Amiel)
- The sting of a reproach is in the truth of it. (Anonymous)
- Truth is heavy; few therefore can bear it. (Hebrew proverb)
- If God were able to backslide from truth, I would fain cling to truth and let God go. (Meister Eckhart)
- Truth is a spectre that scares many. (Anonymous)
- Truth comes in at the window when enquiry is denied at the door. (Benjamin Jowett)

- A half truth is a whole lie. (Yiddish proverb)
- Error is none the better for being common, nor truth the worse for being neglected. (John Locke)
- Truthful lips last for ever, but a lying tongue endures but for a moment. (Proverbs 12:19)
- You will know the truth, and the truth will set you free. (John 8:32)

On goodness

- Better good afar off than evil at hand. (Anonymous)
- Goodness is something so simple: Always live for others, never seek one's own advantage. (Dag Hammarskjöld)
- One good deed atones for a thousand bad ones. (Chinese proverb)
- There is so much good in the worst of us, and so much bad in the best of us, that it behoves all of us not to talk about the rest of us. (Robert Louis Stevenson)
- If there is any good in you, believe there is much more in others. (Anonymous)
- It is not only what we do, but also what we do not do, for which we are accountable. (Molière)
- The first condition of human goodness is something to love; the second, something to reverence. (George Eliot)
- Most people are not as bad as they pretend to be, or as bad as their enemies paint them. (Morris Abram)
- One does evil enough when one does nothing good. (German proverb)
- I have believed the best of every man, and find that to believe it is enough to make a bad man show him at his best, or even the good man swing his lantern higher. (W. B. Yeats)
- Good people's words yield good fruit to eat, but the deceitful hunger only to do more wrong. (Proverbs 13:2)
- Those who are good to others find reward in doing so, whereas those who are cruel ultimately hurt themselves. (Proverbs 11:17)

On faith

- I do not want merely to possess a faith; I want a faith that possesses me. (Charles Kingsley)
- If we really believe in something, we have no choice but to go further. (Graham Greene)
- Faith is never identical with piety. (Karl Barth)
- A faith that cannot survive collision with the truth is not worth many regrets. (Arthur C. Clarke)
- You can do very little with faith, but you can do nothing without it. (Nicholas Murray Butler)

- 'Tis not the dying for a faith that's so hard; 'tis the living up to it. (Thackeray)

- Pray devoutly, but hammer stoutly. (Anonymous)

- There is no love without hope, no hope without love, and neither hope nor love without faith. (St Augustine of Hippo)

- Ultimately, faith is the only key to the universe. The final meaning of human existence, and the answers to the questions on which all our happiness depends cannot be found in any other way. (Thomas Merton)

- It is love makes faith, not faith love. (Cardinal Newman)

- Now faith is confidence concerning things we hope for, unshakable trust in what we do not yet see. (Hebrews 11:1)

- We walk guided not by the things we see but by faith. (2 Corinthians 5:7)

On doubt

- The first key to wisdom is assiduous and frequent questioning. For by doubting we come to inquiry and by inquiry we arrive at truth. (Peter Abelard)

- Who knows nothing, doubts nothing. (French proverb)

- Faith keeps many doubts in her pay. If I could not doubt, I should not believe. (Henry Thoreau)

- There lives more faith in honest doubt . . . than in half the creeds. (Lord Tennyson)

- There are two ways to slide easily through life: to believe everything or to doubt everything; both ways save us from thinking. (Alfred Korzybski)

- Doubt is a pain too lonely to know that faith is its twin brother. (Kahlil Gibran)

- The real atheists are not those who keep asking questions hoping to find a fuller understanding, but those who refuse to ask questions. (Anonymous)

- Feed your faith, and your doubts will starve to death. (Anonymous)

- Never doubt in the dark what God told you in the light. (V. Raymond Edman)

- Deep doubts, deep wisdom; few doubts, little wisdom. (Chinese proverb)

- If you ask, you will receive; if you seek, you will find; if you knock at the door, it will be opened. (Luke 11:9)

- Lord, I believe; help deal with my unbelief. (Mark 9:24b)

On health

- Health is not valued till sickness comes. (English proverb)
- He who has health has hope; and he who has hope has everything. (Arab proverb)
- The sickness of the body may prove the health of the soul. (Author unknown)
- Health and cheerfulness mutually beget each other. (Addison)
- In times of sickness the soul collects itself anew. (Latin proverb)
- He who has health is rich and does not know it. (Italian proverb)
- Sickness shows us what we are. (Latin proverb)
- All sorts of bodily diseases are produced by half-used minds. (George Bernard Shaw)
- I never realised how well I was until I gave up thinking how ill I was. (St Teresa of Avila)
- No one's head aches while comforting another. (Italian proverb)
- Pleasant words resemble honeycomb; they bring sweet refreshment to the soul and promote health of body. (Proverbs 16:24)
- Do not consider yourself wise; instead fear the Lord and renounce evil, for that will bring you healing and refreshment in body, mind and soul. (Proverbs 3:7-8)

On happiness

- True happiness consists in making happy. (Hindi proverb)
- Happiness is not a horse; you cannot harness it. (Chinese/Russian proverb)
- Happiness is not a state to arrive at, but a manner of travelling. (Margaret Lee Runbeck)
- One joy scatters a hundred griefs. (Chinese proverb)
- Joy and sorrow are next-door neighbours. (German proverb)
- Those who bring happiness to the lives of others cannot keep it from themselves. (J. M. Barrie)
- When we cannot find contentment in ourselves it is useless to seek it elsewhere. (La Rochefoucald)
- The supreme happiness of life is the conviction of being loved for yourself, or, more correctly, of being loved in spite of yourself. (Victor Hugo)
- A happiness that is sought for ourselves alone can never be found; for a happiness that is diminished by being shared is not big enough to make us happy. (Thomas Merton)
- Joy is the echo of God's life within us. (Joseph Marmion)
- Those whose strength and confidence lies in the Lord their God, the God of Jacob, will be happy. (Psalm 146:5)
- Happy are those who trust in God. (Proverbs 16:20b)

On wisdom

- Experience is the mother of wisdom. (Anonymous)
- It is a great point of wisdom to find out one's own folly. (Anonymous)
- They have good judgement who rely not wholly on their own. (Anonymous)
- The wise read both books and life itself. (Lin Yutang)
- Wisdom is oftentimes nearer when we stoop than when we soar. (William Wordsworth)
- There is often wisdom under a shabby cloak. (Latin proverb)
- Study without reflection is a waste of time; reflection without study is dangerous. (Confucius)
- The most exquisite folly is made of wisdom spun too fine. (Benjamin Franklin)
- Thinking is the essence of wisdom. (Persian proverb)
- Arrogance diminishes wisdom. (Arabian proverb)
- The root of wisdom lies in fearing God; all who do that will have true insight. (Psalm 111:10)
- Seek teaching rather than silver, knowledge instead of even the purest gold; for wisdom is finer than jewellery, nothing you may wish for is in any way comparable to it. (Proverbs 8:10-11)

On God

- Concerning God, our safest eloquence is silence. (Richard Hooker)
- Do not seek God in outer space – your heart is the only place in which to meet him face to face. (Angelus Silesius)
- A comprehended God is no God. (St John Chrysostom)
- Ever since God created humans in his own image, they have been trying to repay the compliment. (Voltaire)
- Anyone . . . who offers to God a second place offers him no place. (John Ruskin)
- One cannot talk about God merely by talking about man in a loud voice. (Karl Barth)
- The best way to know God is to love many things. (Van Gogh)
- God often visits us, but most of the time we are not at home. (French proverb)
- The atheist staring from his attic window is often nearer to God that the believer caught up in his own false image of God. (Martin Buber)
- We expect too much of God, but he always seems ready. (John F. Kennedy)
- God is a good worker, but he loves to be helped. (Anonymous)

- God is not an idea, or a definition that we have committed to memory; he is a presence which we experience in our hearts. (Louis Evely)
- We know God easily if we do not constrain ourselves to define him. (Joseph Joubert)
- If you don't find God in the very next person you meet, it is a waste of time looking any further. (Mahatma Gandhi)
- God is our sanctuary and our strength, a proven help in times of turmoil, so we will fear nothing, no matter how the world might change. (Psalm 46:1-2a)
- Anyone who fails to love does not know God, for God is love. (1 John 4:8)

Other proverbs/sayings/quips can be found in the following:
- *Quips and Quotes* (H. J. Richards)
- *More Quips and Quotes* (H. J. Richards)
- *Quotes and Anecdotes* (Tony Castle)
- *A Treasury of Christian Wisdom* (Tony Castle, published by Hodder & Stoughton)
- *The Penguin Dictionary of Proverbs* (collected by Rosalind Fergusson)
- *The Oxford Dictionary of Quotations* (Elizabeth Knowles, Oxford University Press)

Suggested music

No special music suggests itself for this service.

Suggested hymns

- Immortal, invisible, God only wise
- The wise man
- God moves in a mysterious way
- Lead us, heavenly Father, lead us
- Teach me, my God and King
- May the mind of Christ my Saviour
- God be in my head

Introduction

All of us, I suspect, will have our own favourite proverbs or sayings, words that for us encapsulate important truths about life. Most of these will have been handed down across innumerable generations, having been familiar to us even as children. You know the kind of thing: 'Too many cooks spoil the broth'; 'Many hands make light work'; 'A rolling stone gathers no moss'; 'A bird in the hand is worth two in a bush'; 'A stitch in time saves nine' – and so we could go on. Who hasn't heard those proverbs, and countless others like them? They are part of our national consciousness, of received wisdom from time immemorial, and few if any would dispute that they do indeed contain simple but profound wisdom. Not academic knowledge or technical learning, but an understanding of how life works, acquired through experience.

Such wisdom finds a significant place in the Bible, both in the book of Proverbs and that of Ecclesiastes, true insight never despised there but celebrated as a gift from God. Today, in place of a talk or sermon, we will hear a selection of sayings and proverbs; words of wisdom on ten different themes taken from books of the Bible, from thinkers and philosophers across the ages and across faiths and cultures, and from the teaching of Jesus. Listen, ponder, pray and ask yourself what God is saying to you through them, what message of hope, challenge, comfort, encouragement or assurance he is offering today.

Suggested readings

Bible verses are included in the list of proverbs/sayings above. If you want a longer reading, any passage from the first five chapters of Proverbs would be appropriate, as would 1 Corinthians 1:26-31.

Prayers

Praise
Lord of all,
　　we acknowledge again today
　　that your ways are not our ways,
　　nor your thoughts our thoughts.
We recognise that what *we* count as wisdom
　　is all too often foolishness,
　　whereas what looks to us like folly can,
　　in your hands,
　　be wisdom beyond words.
Immortal,
　　invisible,
　　God only wise,
　　receive our praise.

We acknowledge you as Alpha and Omega,
　　mighty and mysterious,
　　beyond our understanding;
　　our minds left reeling before your greatness,
　　waiting for the day when what we glimpse now in part
　　we will finally see face to face
　　and know in full.
Immortal,
　　invisible,
　　God only wise,
　　receive our praise.

We acknowledge the awesomeness of your love in Christ,
　　shown so powerfully in the agony and awfulness of the cross –
　　a stumbling block to some and nonsense to others,

but to us power and wisdom,
strength and salvation,
victory and vindication of your gracious purpose.
Immortal,
invisible,
God only wise,
receive our praise.

We acknowledge the wonder of your call to discipleship,
the amazing truth that you love and value us as we are,
delighting in our worship
and taking pleasure in our service,
despite all our weakness,
faults,
doubt
and folly.
Immortal,
invisible,
God only wise,
receive our praise.

Lord of all,
sovereign,
supreme,
we come to listen,
to learn,
to acknowledge,
to adore.
Immortal,
invisible,
God only wise,
receive our praise.

In the name of Christ.
Amen.

Thanksgiving
For wisdom gained by experience,
eternal God,
receive our thanks.

For wisdom accumulated by study,
eternal God,
receive our thanks.

For wisdom passed on by parents,
eternal God,
receive our thanks.

For wisdom handed down across generations,
    eternal God,
    receive our thanks.

For wisdom of other cultures, faiths and philosophies,
    eternal God,
    receive our thanks.

For wisdom acquired through your word,
    eternal God,
    receive our thanks.

For wisdom shared through times of fellowship,
    eternal God,
    receive our thanks.

For wisdom seen in the folly of the cross,
    eternal God,
    receive our thanks.

For wisdom inculcated by your Spirit,
    eternal God,
    receive our thanks.

For wisdom cultivated through knowing,
    fearing
    and loving you.
    eternal God,
    receive our thanks.
Amen.

Confession

Gracious God,
    we know that to fear, honour and serve you
    is the beginning of wisdom,
    yet such knowledge reminds us all too painfully
    of how far we fall short,
    how weak and foolish we continue to be.
For all the ways we fail you,
    Lord, have mercy.

We have confused the wisdom of this world
    with your values,
    imagining that the goals society pursues
    coincide with yours.
We have lost sight of the need to deny ourselves,
    to put the interests of others before our own,
    to love and go on loving,
    to seek treasure in heaven rather than here on earth.

For all the ways we fail you,
   Lord, have mercy.

We have confused our own ideas with your truth,
   assuming that what we don't understand cannot be real,
   what clashes with the view we have of the world
   must be wrong,
   what doesn't accord with our wishes
   can safely be put to one side,
   yet you are a God whose word brings challenge,
   testing,
   teaching,
   transforming.
For all the ways we fail you,
   Lord, have mercy.

We have failed to respond to your guidance,
   to honour you as you deserve,
   to respect your commandments
   or to live as your people.
Time and again we have gone astray,
   losing sight of your purpose
   and belying the faith we profess.
For all the ways we fail you,
   Lord, have mercy.

Open our minds to your word,
   our hearts to your love,
   our souls to your presence
   and our lives to your power,
   so that we might walk in your way
   this day and always,
   through Jesus Christ our Lord.
Amen.

Intercession
Eternal God,
   we bring before you our world in all its need,
   praying especially for those entrusted with offering leadership,
   giving guidance,
   providing instruction
   or affording care –
   their decisions and actions inevitably affecting people's lives
   for better or worse.
In all the complexities of this life,
   grant wisdom to discern the right path.

We pray for leaders of nations,
    politicians
    and local councillors –
    those given the privilege but also daunting responsibility
    of representing others.
In all the complexities of this life,
    grant wisdom to discern the right path.

We pray for judges,
    barristers
    and lawyers,
    their rulings and judgements
    potentially having far-reaching consequences.
In all the complexities of this life,
    grant wisdom to discern the right path.

We pray for teachers and classroom assistants,
    professors and lecturers,
    playgroup leaders and those involved in special education –
    those charged with imparting the precious gifts
    of knowledge and understanding.
In all the complexities of this life,
    grant wisdom to discern the right path.

We pray for clergy,
    counsellors
    and therapists –
    all who strive to offer spiritual succour,
    pastoral support,
    peace of mind
    and inner wholeness.
In all the complexities of this life,
    grant wisdom to discern the right path.

We pray for doctors,
    nurses,
    surgeons
    and specialists –
    all who work in any way to bring help and healing,
    care and rehabilitation.
In all the complexities of this life,
    grant wisdom to discern the right path.

We pray finally for society as a whole,
    in our own country and across the world:
    East and West,
    Christian and non-Christian,
    rich and poor,

young and old –
so much that divides
but so much more that unites if only we will see;
so much that is evil
but so much also that is good.
In all the complexities of this life,
grant wisdom to discern the right path.

Eternal God,
hear our prayer,
in the name of Christ.
Amen.

Closing prayer
In our foolishness be our wisdom,
in our confusion be our guide,
in our darkness be our light,
in our errors be our truth.
Lead us in your way, O Lord,
this day and always.
Amen.

Order of Service

The proverbs and sayings in this service are designed to speak for themselves, so no place has been given for a sermon or talk.

- Key verses
- Introduction
- Hymn
- Prayer of praise
- Proverbs and sayings
  On truth
  On doubt
  On goodness
- Hymn
- Prayer of thanksgiving
- Proverbs and sayings
  On faith
  On hope
  On love
- Prayer of confession

- Hymn
- Proverbs and sayings
  On health
  On happiness
  On wisdom
  On God
- Prayer of intercession
- Hymn
- Closing prayer

QUIZZES

23 So much more to learn

A service using quiz questions to highlight that our faith should always be growing, exploring new horizons

The aim of this service is to emphasise that there is always more to discover about God's goodness and grace, faith constantly needing to grow.

Key verses

I pray for this . . . that Christ may so dwell in your hearts through faith that you will be able to grasp with all the saints the breadth, length, height and depth of the love of Christ, and that you may know this all-surpassing love in such a way that you will be filled with the very fullness of God!
Ephesians 3:14a, 17-19

When I was a child I thought and reasoned like a child; when I reached adulthood I put a stop to childish ways. At present we see only in part, as though looking through smoked glass; then we shall see face to face. Now we see only in part; then we will know fully, just as we are fully known.
1 Corinthians 13:11-12

Resources

• This service, suitable for an all-age service or adults only, makes use of quiz questions – many of them purposely difficult – to bring home that, however much we know, there are always gaps in our knowledge. A variety of quizzes are set out below:

Quiz 1
The following can be used in three different ways: (a) you could ask people to identify what each of the following scientific disciplines studies (i.e. what does an abiologist study?); (b) you could turn the question round and ask who studies the various subjects (i.e. what do we call the study of inanimate objects?); or (c) you could print off the various disciplines and subjects on separate pieces of card/paper, jumbling them up on a board and asking the congregation if they can match the discipline to the subject.

Abiology	Inanimate objects
Anemology	Winds
Apiology	Bees
Cartology	Map-making
Cetology	Whales
Cryology	Snow and ice
Cynology	Dogs
Dendrology	Trees

Fromology	Cheese
Graphology	Handwriting
Hippology	Horses
Orology	Mountains
Philology	Languages
Pistology	Faith
Pyrology	Fire and heat
Trichology	Hair and hair diseases
Virology	Viruses
Xylology	Wood

Quiz 2

Ask the congregation who is credited with being the first to invent, discover, reach or develop the following (the answers are given in italics):

South Pole	*Roald Amundsen*
Telephone	*Alexander Graham Bell*
Scissors (en masse)	*Robert Hinchcliffe*
The compass	*Petrus Peregrinus de Maricourt*
Circulation of blood	*Sir William Harvey*
Gravity	*Isaac Newton*
Theory of relativity	*Albert Einstein*
Cardiac pacemaker	*Dr Ake Senning*
Electric telegraph	*Samuel Morse*
Coca-Cola	*Dr John Pemberton*
Miner's safety lamp	*Sir Humphry Davy*
Spectacles	*Salvino degli Armati and his friend Alessandro della Spina*
Steam engine	*Thomas Savery*
Submarine	*David Bushnell*
Miniskirt	*Mary Quant*
Television	*John Logie Baird*
Flush toilet	*Sir John Harington*
Australia	*James Cook*
Meccano	*Frank Hornby*
Post-it notes	*Dr Spencer Sylver*
Penicillin	*Alexander Fleming*
Magnifying glass	*Roger Bacon*
Jet engine	*Sir Frank Whittle*
Waterproof rubber	*Sir Charles Macintosh*
Dynamite	*Alfred Nobel*
Revolver	*Samuel Colt*
Trivial Pursuit®	*Chris and John Haney and Scott Abbott*
Typewriter	*Pelegrino Turri*
Crossword puzzle	*Arthur Wynne*

Quiz 3

Test the congregation's knowledge of capital cities. Again, you might follow one of the three methods of presentation outlined for Quiz 1.

Iceland	Reykjavik
Macedonia	Skopje
Cuba	Havana
Malta	Valletta
Fiji	Suva
Austria	Vienna
Australia	Canberra
Latvia	Riga
Bangladesh	Dhaka
Ethiopia	Addis Ababa
Ghana	Accra
Indonesia	Jakarta
Vietnam	Hanoi
Albania	Tirana
Morocco	Rabat
Sudan	Khartoum
Uganda	Kampala
Bosnia	Sarajevo
Zambia	Lusaka
Chile	Santiago
Peru	Lima
Liechtenstein	Vaduz
Bolivia	La Paz
Lithuania	Vilnius
Greenland	Nuuk
Colombia	Bogotá
Uruguay	Montevideo

Quiz 4

Ask the congregation to answer the following without cheating (the answers are in italics; those using the Roman Catholic canon will need to adjust some of the questions):

How many books of the Bible are there? *66*
Which book comes after 2 Kings? *1 Chronicles*
Which books come before and after Ruth? *Judges and 1 Samuel*
How many verses are there in Psalm 119? *176*
How many chapters are there in the book of Ezekiel? *48*
What is the closing word of the Old Testament? *curse*
How many chapters are there in the book of Philemon? *1*
Which book comes between Ecclesiastes and Isaiah? *Song of Solomon*
What is the closing word of the New Testament? *Amen*
How many books of the Bible begin with the letter 'M'? *4*

How do you spell Habakkuk?   *As seen*
What are the first five books of the Old Testament?
                    Genesis, Exodus, Leviticus, Numbers, Deuteronomy
What are the last five books of the Old Testament?
                    Habakkuk, Zephaniah, Haggai, Zechariah, Malachi
How many books of the Bible begin with the letter 'J' –
(ignore any numbers before the 'J')?   *12*
What are the opening words of the New Testament?
                              An account of the genealogy . . .
How many letters to the Colossians did Paul write?   *1*
What book comes between Jeremiah and Ezekiel?   *Lamentations*
What are the first five books of the New Testament?
                    Matthew, Mark, Luke, John, Acts of the Apostles
What are the last five books of the New Testament? (NRSV)
                    1, 2 and 3 John, Jude, Revelation
Which books come before and after Titus?   *2 Timothy and Philemon*
How many chapters are there in the book of Romans?   *16*
Which book comes after Nehemiah?   *Esther*
Which book comes before Hebrews?   *Philemon*
How many verses are there in the book of Jude?   *25*
How many books of the Bible begin with the letter 'E'?   *5*

Suggested hymns
- O God of all creation
- We limit not the truth of God
- Help us, O Lord, to learn
- Lord, there are times when I have to ask 'Why?'
- Lord, that I may learn
- Through the night of doubt and sorrow
- More about Jesus would I know

Introduction

How much do we know of God? Whatever the answer to that question, of one thing we can be certain: there is far more that we don't know. Our knowledge of any subject, no matter how expert we may be, is partial; with God it is necessarily even more so. Today, through various quizzes, we are going to remind ourselves of that important truth, and so commit ourselves to a continuing journey of discipleship.

Suggested readings
- Romans 11:33-36
- Ephesians 3:16-19
- 1 Corinthians 13:11-12

Talk précis

The more we know, it is sometimes said, the more we realise we have yet to learn. And the converse of that, of course, is the old saying 'A little knowledge is a dangerous thing'. Both are spot on, aren't they? All too easily we pick up a snippet about a subject here and there, and imagine we know it all, blundering into conversations in which we succeed only in exposing how little we have actually understood. Not only can this prove embarrassing, it can also hurt us and others if we base decisions or judgements on our flimsy grasp of a situation or subject. By contrast, when we truly delve into a topic, whatever it might be, we discover aspects, implications, possibilities and nuances that we'd not even begun to consider, and we realise that our knowledge can never be fully complete, for the boundaries of understanding are forever being extended.

If that's true of knowledge in general, how much more so must it necessarily be of God, the one who is greater than our minds can fully comprehend, who defies definition, who is before all, within all and beyond all. When it comes to faith there is always further to grow, more to understand, new avenues to be explored. If we imagine there isn't, then we have gone sadly wrong. Today, through easy and not-so-easy questions, we remind ourselves of that vital fact; however far we have progressed on our pilgrimage of faith, the journey is not yet complete.

Prayers   *Praise*
Almighty God,
    enthroned in splendour,
    we have come together to worship you,
    to offer,
    as best we are able,
    our humble homage
    and joyful adoration.
Nothing begins to express your glory.
In awe and wonder, we honour you.

Your love is wider than the widest ocean,
    deeper than the deepest sea,
    higher than the highest mountain.
Nothing begins to express your glory.
In awe and wonder, we honour you.

Your grace shines more surely than the brightest star,
    flows more freely than the fastest river,
    bubbles more truly than the clearest spring.
Nothing begins to express your glory.
In awe and wonder, we honour you.

Your power is greater than the fiercest earthquake,
    stronger than the wildest storm,
    grander than the mightiest empire.
Nothing begins to express your glory.
In awe and wonder, we honour you.

Your peace is purer than the whitest dove,
   lighter than the softest touch,
   kinder than the gentlest breeze.
Nothing begins to express your glory.
In awe and wonder, we honour you.

Your goodness is richer than the costliest treasure,
   sweeter than the finest honey,
   lovelier than the loveliest flower.
Nothing begins to express your glory.
In awe and wonder, we honour you.

Almighty God,
   words fail us in your presence,
   for none can do you justice.
Whatever metaphors we use,
   whatever superlatives we employ,
   at best, they can merely hint at the truth,
   pointing feebly towards the breathtaking reality beyond –
   the wonder of all you are
   and all you do.
Nothing begins to express your glory.
In awe and wonder, we honour you.

Speak to us now,
   so that we may grasp a little more fully how great you are,
   and recognise yet more clearly how much we still have to learn.
In Christ's name we ask it.
Amen.

Thanksgiving

For all we learn of you from your word,
   Lord,
   we thank you.

For all we learn of you through prayer,
   Lord,
   we thank you.

For all we learn of you in our daily relationships,
   Lord,
   we thank you.

For all we learn of you from the testimony of others,
   Lord,
   we thank you.

For all we learn of you through your Spirit's prompting,
   Lord,
   we thank you.

For all we learn of you in times of quiet contemplation,
   Lord,
   we thank you.

For all we learn of you from the wonder of creation,
   Lord,
   we thank you.

For all we learn of you through the example of Christ,
   Lord,
   we thank you.

For all we learn of you in times of worship,
   Lord,
   we thank you.

For all we learn of you from your still small voice within,
   Lord,
   we thank you.

For all we learn of you through the fellowship we share,
   Lord,
   we thank you.

For all we learn of you in ways too many to number.
   Lord,
   we thank you.

For the fact that our knowledge of you never stands still,
   but is constantly being expanded,
   enriched,
   refashioned
   and renewed.
   Lord,
   we thank you.
Amen.

Confession
Gracious God,
   among our many failings
   we have forgotten our need to learn more of you
   and to grow in faith.
For minds that have been closed to your Spirit,
   Lord, have mercy.

We have been complacent about our relationship with you,
    leaving it to you to make all the running,
    imagining that we need only to sit back and receive,
    to snap our fingers and find you there at our beck and call.
For minds that have been closed to your Spirit,
    Lord, have mercy.

We have been arrogant in our attitude,
    assuming that our experience is normative,
    our convictions correct
    and our assumptions unassailable;
    that our ability to understand is a measure of truth.
For minds that have been closed to your Spirit,
    Lord, have mercy.

We have been lazy,
    failing to make time to study your word,
    to pray,
    worship
    or reflect,
    devotion pushed to the periphery of daily life.
For minds that have been closed to your Spirit,
    Lord, have mercy.

We have been cowardly,
    afraid that knowing you better
    or exploring our faith more deeply
    might lead us into uncharted waters,
    so that we find ourselves all at sea,
    unsure whether we will sink or swim.
For minds that have been closed to your Spirit,
    Lord, have mercy.

We have been distracted,
    allowing other pleasures,
    other responsibilities,
    other needs
    and other interests
    to come between us
    and to prevent us considering the things that really matter.
For minds that have been closed to your Spirit,
    Lord, have mercy.

Gracious God,
    teach us that, whoever we are
    and wherever we may have reached
    in the journey of discipleship,

there is and always will be so much more to learn,
and give us a hunger, each day,
to know you better
and to grow in understanding of your loving purpose,
through Jesus Christ our Lord.
Amen.

Intercession
Living God,
hear our prayer for all those entrusted with imparting learning –
that they may recognise the importance of their work
and be equipped to discharge it faithfully.
By your grace, Lord,
may minds be opened to greater truths
and lives to deeper discernment.

We pray for those in our playgroups, schools, colleges and universities –
teachers, classroom assistants, lecturers and professors;
give them the skill they need to communicate,
inspire,
instruct,
elucidate.
By your grace, Lord,
may minds be opened to greater truths
and lives to deeper discernment.

We pray for those involved in special needs and adult education;
give them perceptiveness,
dedication,
skill
and sensitivity.
By your grace, Lord,
may minds be opened to greater truths
and lives to deeper discernment.

We pray for clergy, Sunday school teachers,
and all others given a teaching ministry
within the life of the Church;
give them insight,
vision,
commitment
and the guidance of your Spirit in all they do and say.
By your grace, Lord,
may minds be opened to greater truths
and lives to deeper discernment.

We pray for those in places of work entrusted with training,
     mentoring,
     supervising
     and apprenticing,
     passing on skills
     and helping to develop new ones;
     give them patience,
     perseverance
     and enthusiasm.
By your grace, Lord,
     may minds be opened to greater truths
     and lives to deeper discernment.

We pray for those who constantly strive
     to push back the boundaries of knowledge –
     researchers,
     students,
     scholars,
     scientists;
     give them wisdom,
     discernment,
     diligence
     and determination.
By your grace, Lord,
     may minds be opened to greater truths
     and lives to deeper discernment.

We pray also for those who feel they cannot learn,
     prevented from doing so by limited ability,
     lack of resources,
     or the need to focus on more immediate concerns;
     give them encouragement,
     support,
     resolve
     and opportunity.
By your grace, Lord,
     may minds be opened to greater truths
     and lives to deeper discernment.

We pray finally for those who no longer seek to learn,
     imagining that their understanding is complete,
     their knowledge sufficient,
     or their grasp of things enough to get them by;
     give them humility,
     open-mindedness
     and a renewed spirit of enquiry.
By your grace, Lord,

**may minds be opened to greater truths
and lives to deeper discernment.**

Living God,
   hear this and all our prayers,
   through Jesus Christ our Lord.
Amen.

Closing prayer
Today and every day, Lord,
   open our minds to everything you have yet to say,
   yet to teach
   and yet to reveal,
   through Jesus Christ our Lord.
Amen.

**Order of
Service**

- Key verses
- Introduction
- Hymn
- Prayer of praise
- Quiz 1
- Reading
- Hymn
- Quiz 2
- Prayer of thanksgiving
- Hymn
- Quiz 3
- Talk
- Prayer of confession
- Hymn
- Quiz 4
- Prayer of intercession
- Hymn
- Closing prayer

24 Any questions?

*A fun service exploring the need to use the mind
as well as the heart in responding to Christ*

The aim of this service is to emphasise that doubt and questions are an integral part of a living and growing faith.

Key verse

If you ask, you will receive; if you seek, you will find; if you knock at the door, it will be opened.
Luke 11:9

Resources

- This service revolves around the old radio show *Twenty Questions*. If you haven't encountered this before, the aim is very simple. Volunteers think of an object, person or bird/animal, etc., and the panel has to guess what or who this is through asking various questions, these phrased in such a way that they can be answered 'yes' or 'no', the only two answers allowed. Once 20 questions have been asked, the panel is defeated and the answer revealed. The only resource needed, then, is individuals primed to take part (having decided beforehand on the object, person, bird/animal to be guessed) and the congregation asked to act as the panel. If you think the congregation will be reluctant to ask questions, you may prefer instead to select two teams, well in advance, explaining to them what is involved in the exercise.

Suggested music

- *Blowin' in the wind* (Bob Dylan)
- *Where have all the flowers gone?* (Pete Seeger)

Suggested hymns

- Put all your faith in God's great goodness
- Through the night of doubt and sorrow
- When days are touched with sadness
- Spirit of faith, come down
- Have faith in God, my heart

Introduction

There are more questions than answers, the old ditty has it. For many of us there's at least an element of truth in that when it comes to faith. Partly it's because there are aspects of life that we struggle to reconcile with our faith, but it's also because, as with anything, the more we learn, the more we realise there is still to understand. Just as children are always asking questions in order to make sense of the world around them, so questions are important for us as Christians and play an important part in helping us reach Christian maturity. Today, borrowing an idea from the old BBC radio show *Twenty Questions*, we will be exploring just how useful and important questioning can be in opening up new insights and understanding.

Suggested readings
- Job 42:1-6
- Proverbs 2:1-14
- Luke 11:1-13

Talk précis

One of the things any good teacher will tell you is never be afraid to ask questions. If you don't understand something or if you've only partly grasped it, then it's no use sitting back quietly doing nothing, vainly hoping that a sudden flash of inspiration will make all clear. If something doesn't make sense, then ask for help, seek enlightenment, and keep on badgering away until things become clearer. You may not find the answers you're looking for as quickly as you would like, you may still struggle to grasp certain truths and still at times have to muddle through, living with paradox and apparent contradictions, but if you search for comprehension and keep on asking the questions, you will inexorably discover more as time goes by. We've seen the truth of that illustrated very simply today in our *Twenty Questions* sessions, carefully chosen questions quickly helping to reveal what was previously hidden. The same holds true in the field of science and research, for it is those who are prepared to challenge established ideas, to delve deeper into a subject, to ask questions others are afraid to answer who pave the way for advances in knowledge and understanding, making possible so much of what we take for granted today.

With faith that's as true as anywhere, perhaps all the more so, yet worryingly many give the impression it has no room for questions, doubt being seen as wholly negative, fundamentally incompatible with belief. Does that make any sense? Does it do justice to the height, length, breadth and depth of the God we worship? And can any faith that is not prepared to challenge and enquire truly hope to grow? That's not to say we can ever presume to know all the answers – far from it. Nor is it to suggest that we reject what we do not understand – that would be foolish, for faith by definition has to live with mystery. Just as the scientist has to accept that the fact we cannot account for something doesn't make it less real, so we too, like Job in our reading, must recognise that God is always ultimately beyond us, our minds always struggling to take in even a fraction of truth let alone all: 'I have spoken concerning what I did not grasp, things too wonderful for me to understand, which I could not fathom' (Job 42:3b). Yet that is no reason not to search for understanding; it is simply a reminder that we must do so with humility. As the book of Proverbs put it, 'If you cry out for insight, and raise your voice for understanding, seeking it as for hidden treasure, then you will understand the fear of the Lord and find the knowledge of God. For the Lord gives wisdom; from his mouth come knowledge and understanding' (Proverbs 2:3-6). Are you eager to learn, hungry to grow? Do you have questions, things you don't understand? Then humbly but honestly ask God for enlightenment and keep on searching; seek and you *will* find.

Prayers   *Praise*

Marvellous and mysterious God,
    there is so much we don't understand,
    so much we cannot make sense of,
    but we believe you love us
    and will go on doing so for all eternity.
In that conviction,
    Lord, we praise you.

Awesome and almighty God,
    there is so much that doesn't make sense,
    so much that seems to fly in the face of your purpose,
    but we believe your will shall triumph
    and good finally conquer evil.
In that conviction,
    Lord, we praise you.

Gentle and generous God,
    there is so much in life that disturbs and troubles,
    so much that seems to contradict your goodness,
    yet we believe you can give a peace beyond understanding
    and life in all its fullness.
In that conviction,
    Lord, we praise you.

Caring and compassionate God,
    there is so much suffering and sorrow in our world,
    so much that seems to deny your presence,
    but we believe you care about human suffering
    and long to bring blessing to all.
In that conviction,
    Lord, we praise you.

Renewing and redeeming God,
there is so much wrong in our lives,
    so much that seems undeserving of forgiveness,
    but we believe your nature is always to have mercy,
    to absolve the past and help us start again.
In that conviction,
    Lord, we praise you.

Sovereign and saving God,
    there is so much about the future that frightens us,
    so much that undermines hope and trust,
    but we believe you will give us strength to meet each challenge
    and be with us even beyond death.
In that conviction,
    Lord, we praise you.

Marvellous and majestic God,
    there is so much about you that puzzles and confuses,
    so much about faith we struggle to comprehend,
    but we believe you have revealed yourself in Christ,
    making known your glory in human form.
In that conviction,
    Lord, we praise you.

Living and loving God,
    receive our worship and praise,
    despite our many doubts,
    our many questions,
    for, whatever may not be clear,
    we have glimpsed in you the one who gives meaning to life,
    who meets our deepest needs,
    who satisfies our souls.
In that conviction,
    Lord, we praise you.
Amen.

Thanksgiving

Loving God,
    we thank you that there is so much to explore within faith
    just as there is with life in general.
We thank you that your greatness is such that we can never exhaust it,
    never know all there is to know
    or understand all there is to understand.
For all we have yet to learn,
    yet to discover,
    we bring our grateful worship.

We thank you for those who enquire into faith,
    for theologians, writers and preachers
    who seek to dig more deeply,
    probe more searchingly
    and explore more thoroughly
    into the message of the gospel,
    the testimony of Scripture,
    the story of the Church
    and the nature of belief.
For all we have yet to learn,
    yet to discover,
    we bring our grateful worship.

We thank you for those who ask searching questions
    about daily life,
    and about the affairs and institutions of this world –

those with sufficient courage to challenge what seems wrong,
　　to engage in dialogue with contrasting points of view,
　　and to seek answers where things are not as they should be.
For all we have yet to learn,
　　yet to discover,
　　we bring our grateful worship.

We thank you for those who ask questions of us –
　　who stretch our horizons to consider new ideas,
　　who prompt us to think afresh about our goals and aspirations,
　　who quicken our consciences
　　and who help us to see ourselves as we really are.
For all we have yet to learn,
　　yet to discover,
　　we bring our grateful worship.

We thank you for welcoming the questions we put to you,
　　being eager to lead us into new insights,
　　greater understanding,
　　deeper discipleship
　　and fuller faith.
For all we have yet to learn,
　　yet to discover,
　　we bring our grateful worship.

In Christ's name we pray.
Amen.

Confession

Living God,
　　you tell us in Christ to ask so that we shall receive,
　　to seek so that we shall find,
　　but when it comes to asking about faith,
　　questioning what it all means,
　　we are hesitant,
　　even hostile,
　　uncertain if that has any place in discipleship.
For an undemanding, unenquiring faith,
　　forgive us, O Lord.

We have been *afraid* to ask questions,
　　fearful of where they might lead,
　　of what comfortable preconceptions they might challenge,
　　of what cherished convictions they might threaten,
　　of what questions might be asked of us.
For an undemanding, unenquiring faith,
　　forgive us, O Lord.

We have been *too lazy* to ask questions,
   unwilling to give the time, thought and energy
   needed to explore the mysteries of faith
   and its relationship to the enigmas of life.
For an undemanding, unenquiring faith,
   forgive us, O Lord.

We have been *too busy* to ask questions,
   too concerned with the demands of each day,
   our own interests,
   and much that is ultimately trivial
   to make time to deepen our knowledge of you.
For an undemanding, unenquiring faith,
   forgive us, O Lord.

We have been *cautious* in asking questions,
   concerned that somehow it is unfaithful to you,
   a sign of weakness,
   a betrayal of the Church,
   a letting the side down.
For an undemanding, unenquiring faith,
   forgive us, O Lord.

We have been guilty of asking the *wrong* questions,
   questions that say more about us than you –
   our own weakness,
   selfishness,
   pride
   or narrow horizons.
For an undemanding, unenquiring faith,
   forgive us, O Lord.

We have been *judgemental* of those who ask questions,
   criticising their soundness,
   their commitment,
   their motives,
   their very faith itself.
For an undemanding, unenquiring faith,
   forgive us, O Lord.

Living God,
   teach us to recognise that questions are integral to faith,
   a way of leading us into a deeper relationship with you
   and a richer understanding of your purpose.
Teach us, then, to offer them to you
   not with apologies and embarrassment
   but as an expression of worship
   and token of our commitment –

our yearning to know, love and serve you better,
to the glory of your name.
Amen.

Intercession
All-loving God,
    hear our prayer for those who have more questions than answers,
    the things they cannot make sense of
    threatening to undermine their faith
    or having destroyed it already.
Where life brings puzzles too hard to live with,
    grant answers, O Lord.

We pray for those overcome by tragedy,
    their lives shattered by circumstances affecting themselves
    or their loved ones:
    disease,
    disaster,
    abuse,
    betrayal,
    rape,
    murder,
    bomb
    or bullet.
Where life brings puzzles too hard to live with,
    grant answers, O Lord.

We pray for those crushed by need and poverty,
    their lives overwhelmed by famine,
    flood,
    earthquake,
    storm,
    warfare,
    terrorism,
    injustice
    or corruption.
Where life brings puzzles too hard to live with,
    grant answers, O Lord.

We pray for those yearning to believe,
    searching for faith,
    yet unable to resolve the questions they have –
    events that appear to deny your love
    and issues hard to square with Christian commitment –
    and we pray likewise for those who,
    for similar reasons,
    are struggling to cling on to faith

or whose commitment has grown cold.
Where life brings puzzles too hard to live with,
  grant answers, O Lord.

Loving God,
  answer these and all our prayers
  in the name of Christ.
Amen.

Closing prayer
Journey with us, Lord, on the pilgrimage of faith,
  and teach us to bring all that troubles,
  perplexes
  and confuses us
  freely to you.
Speak through our questions to deepen and enrich our faith,
  through Jesus Christ our Lord.
Amen.

Order of Service

- Key verse
- Introduction
- Hymn
- Prayer of praise
- *Any Questions?* (session 1)
- Hymn
- *Any Questions?* (session 2)
- Reading
- Hymn
- Prayer of thanksgiving
- *Any Questions?* (session 3)
- Talk
- Prayer of confession
- Hymn
- Prayer of intercession
- Hymn
- Closing prayer

PUZZLES

25   Work it out

A fun service emphasising the part we must play in working out our own salvation

The aim of this service is to use fun puzzles to help explore the part we have to play in working out our own salvation.

Key verse

You must work out your own salvation with fear and trembling, recognising that God is at work in you so that you will be able to understand and accomplish his good purpose.
Philippians 2:12

Resources

- For this service you will need a variety of puzzles. Print off some on sheets to hand to members of the congregation as they come in. Enlarge others (either printed off poster-size or via a PowerPoint presentation) ready for use with the whole congregation during the service. Some puzzle ideas are given below.

Puzzle 1: Wordsearch

Print off the letters in the wordsearch below and arrange on a whiteboard using Blu-Tack or magnetic tape. Ask the congregation to find words in the following wordsearch relating to what God has done for us or gives us. (The words are RENEWAL, PARDON, MERCY, LOVE, GRACE, LIFE, SALVATION, SPIRIT, TRUTH, JOY, REDEEMED, FORGIVEN, CHOSEN, PEACE, HOPE, FAITH. Remove each word as it is identified.) Ask what words are left (i.e. GIFTS OF GOD). Each of the words found relates to the part God plays in offering us new life.

G	Y	I	N	O	D	R	A	P	F
R	C	N	T	G	S	L	O	V	E
E	R	E	H	R	A	N	S	T	D
N	E	S	O	A	L	E	S	R	E
E	M	O	P	C	V	V	P	U	M
W	O	H	E	E	A	I	I	T	E
A	F	C	G	O	T	G	R	H	E
L	L	I	F	E	I	R	I	J	D
F	A	I	T	H	O	O	T	O	E
E	C	A	E	P	N	F	D	Y	R

Repeat the procedure with the second wordsearch below. The words this time are COMMITMENT, DEVOTION, SERVICE, DEDICATION, DISCIPLINE, LOYALTY, THANKS, LOVE, WORSHIP, TRUST, OBEDIENCE, PRAISE, and the remaining letters this time spell out OUR RESPONSE; the words found this time relate to the part we must play in helping to work out our salvation; not earning it, but responding to all God has done.

T	N	E	M	T	I	M	M	O	C
O	O	B	E	D	I	E	N	C	E
U	N	O	I	T	O	V	E	D	R
E	N	I	L	P	I	C	S	I	D
R	T	E	T	H	A	N	K	S	S
E	R	Y	T	L	A	Y	O	L	P
V	U	O	S	E	R	V	I	C	E
O	S	N	E	S	I	A	R	P	S
L	T	W	O	R	S	H	I	P	E
D	E	D	I	C	A	T	I	O	N

Puzzle 2: Spot the difference
Spot the 11 differences between the following two pictures

The differences are as follows: different pattern on flag, different time on clock, different-shaped side door, different bar on the third window from the right, different pattern on small window in lean-to section, different-size and shaped clouds, different number of birds, different arm positions for person by tower, different handles on right door, different roof tiles, door handle added on side door in second picture.

Puzzle 3: Anagram
Ask the congregation if they can work out what the following cryptic message is in fact an anagram of:

AS TRIAL OK YOU NOW VOW TO RUN

Answer: Work out your own salvation

Puzzle 4: Hangman
Invite the congregation to play 'Hangman', allowing one guess per person. Explain that rather than one word you have prepared a whole phrase (the answer is 'CAN YOU WORK THIS OUT'):

_ _ _   _ _ _   _ _ _ _   _ _ _ _   _ _ _

Puzzle 5: Cracking the code
Ask if anyone can crack the code you've used to discover the hidden message below:

XLI PSVH LEW CIX QSVI PMKLX ERH XVYXL XS FVIEO JSVXL JVSQ LMW ASVH

(Answer: THE LORD HAS YET MORE LIGHT AND TRUTH TO BREAK FORTH FROM HIS WORD – i.e. for each letter of the original count back four letters in the alphabet, going back to the end of the alphabet if necessary.)

Suggested hymns

• Will you come and follow me?
• May the mind of Christ my Saviour
• Lord Jesus Christ
• O for a closer walk with God
• Dear Master, in whose life I see
• Breathe on me, Breath of God
• More about Jesus would I know
• When we walk with the Lord
• O Jesus Christ, grow thou in me
• When my love to Christ grows weak
• Don't let my love grow cold
• O loving Lord, who art for ever seeking
• We have not known thee as we ought

Introduction

Our service today is designed to get you thinking. It revolves around puzzles, each of which you have to work out for yourselves. Hopefully you'll find it fun, but hopefully also you'll glimpse behind it a deeper message concerning faith. We'll come to it in more detail later, though perhaps by the time we get there it will simply be a question of emphasising what you've already understood; what, to put it another way, you will already have worked out for yourselves.

Suggested readings

• Matthew 16:13-17
• Philippians 2:12-18
• Ephesians 6:10-20

Talk précis

What does faith or being a Christian have to do with the various puzzles we've tackled today? In one sense the answer is nothing: God does not set out to trip us up, nor is faith in any way dependent on our own ingenuity or some special knowledge. But in another sense those puzzles have everything to do with faith, for they remind us what is involved in doing as Paul suggests and working out our own salvation.

First, we need to work out *our own* salvation; in other words, when it comes to coming to faith, responding to God, no one else can do it for us. Knowing God is a personal thing. We cannot inherit faith or borrow commitment by proxy, still less learn it parrot-fashion. We cannot consider ourselves a Christian because we know about Jesus and have heard something of the gospel, or because we live in a Christian country, or because we have some vague belief in God. True faith comes down to an ongoing relationship with God in Christ. That surely is the point of Paul's words to the Philippians. He wasn't implying in any way that we can earn our salvation or that finding it in some way depends on our efforts or ingenuity. Rather, we must work it out for ourselves. Compare, for example, working out a sum for oneself and doing it on a calculator. Using the latter method we may get the answer right every time, but we'd never really understand how we got there. Without the calculator we'd be lost. Similarly, consider learning to ride a bike. We can be taught the theory so that we know exactly what to do, but unless we actually get up on the saddle and start pedalling we don't really know how to cycle. It's only when we do something or work it out for ourselves that we really understand what's involved.

Secondly, Paul wants to stress how vital it is that we *work at* our relationship with God, that we play our part in nurturing and sustaining faith, striving as best we can to become more like Christ. Like any other relationship, if ours with God is to be all it should be and not ultimately to founder, it needs us to put something in, to give time to it, to play our part in building it up. Only thus can we get to know God better. Yes, we are ultimately dependent on grace, justified by faith alone, but that does not mean we can sit back and leave everything to God. True faith entails commitment offered in joyful response to all he has done. Neglect that, imagine that faith can take care of itself, and we will swiftly find that it shrivels up and dies.

Do it for yourself, work it out for yourself – it's a good lesson to learn about life; equally good to learn about faith. Are we taking Paul's challenge as seriously as we should?

Prayers   *Praise*
Loving God,
   we praise you for valuing us as individuals,
   for seeing us not as part of some nameless crowd,
   nor merely as part of your Church,
   but as your children,
   each of us unique,
   precious in your sight
   and of infinite worth and significance.
For welcoming and cherishing us as we are,
   we honour you, O Lord.

We praise you that you want us to know you for ourselves,
   to enter into a living personal relationship with you,
   conscious of your presence,
   your nearness,
   your hand upon us,
   and your Spirit within –
   a God we can walk and talk with.
For welcoming and cherishing us as we are,
   we honour you, O Lord.

We praise you that you do not treat us as puppets,
   imposing your will on us
   and controlling our footsteps,
   but that you give us instead free will,
   the responsibility of making our own decisions
   and the ability to respond to you in our own way.
For welcoming and cherishing us as we are,
   we honour you, O Lord.

We praise you that we are all different
   and that you deal with us accordingly,
   each having diverse experiences of your love,
   varying insights into your purpose,
   and contrasting ways of worshipping, serving
   and understanding you,
   all having something to learn from one another
   and something to share.
For welcoming and cherishing us as we are,
   we honour you, O Lord.

Loving God,
   help us to make the most of our freedom,
   our uniqueness,
   and the welcome you so graciously extend,
   so that we may grow as people,
   grow in faith,
   and grow closer to you each day,
   through Jesus Christ our Lord.
Amen.

Thanksgiving
Lord Jesus Christ,
   for loving us so much that you died for us,
   in gratitude
   we worship you.

For revealing the grace and truth of the sovereign saving God,
   in gratitude
   we worship you.

For offering rest for our weary souls,
   relief from carrying our heavy burdens,
   in gratitude
   we worship you.

For giving light to our path
   and a lamp to our feet,
   in gratitude
   we worship you.

For seeking us when we were lost
   and loving us despite our many faults and failings,
   in gratitude
   we worship you.

For winning us life in all its fullness,
   life now and for all eternity,
   in gratitude
   we worship you.

For calling us not servants but friends,
   able to respond to you and know you for ourselves,
   in gratitude
   we worship you.

For sending your Spirit to teach, comfort,
   encourage, inspire,
   in gratitude
   we worship you.

For your word of life,
   reinforced through all you did and continue to do,
   in gratitude
   we worship you.

For the opportunity freely to respond
   and to play our part in the work of your kingdom,
   in gratitude
   we worship you.

Lord Jesus Christ,
   we thank you for the wonder of knowing you
   and the joy of salvation.
Teach us to treasure and nurture your gift

so that our lives may reflect *our* gratitude
and *your* glory,
now and always.
In Christ's name we pray.
Amen.

Confession
Great and wonderful God,
we talk about a living relationship with you,
about responding to and knowing you one to one,
but so often the reality is otherwise.
For our fractured faith
and careless discipleship,
Lord, forgive us.

We have not spent time with you as we should,
more often than not scarcely giving you a second thought.
We have been neglectful of devotion,
erratic in prayer
and forgetful of your word,
our Sunday worship kept apart from daily life.
For our fractured faith
and careless discipleship,
Lord, forgive us.

We have thought little about what discipleship means,
rarely taking stock of our lives,
seldom seeking to grow in grace
and more infrequently still witnessing to your love in Christ.
We have been closet Christians,
seeing discipleship as a private matter
that we dip into as the mood takes us.
For our fractured faith
and careless discipleship,
Lord, forgive us.

We have left everything to you,
believing that faith alone,
however tenuous,
is all we need,
forgetting that, though works can never earn salvation,
our life in Christ should nonetheless bear fruit,
and that we have a part to play in helping that to happen.
For our fractured faith
and careless discipleship,
Lord, forgive us.

Teach us what it means to work out our salvation –
　　above all, through working *at* our relationship with you,
　　at our commitment to Christ
　　and at the service we offer in his name.
Teach us to make time for you
　　as you have made time for us.
In his name we pray.
Amen.

Intercession
Saving God,
　　hear our prayer for all who proclaim the gospel
　　and all who have responded.
Speak your word of life,
　　your word of love.

We pray for evangelists,
　　ministers,
　　pastors,
　　teachers –
　　all who speak *of* you
　　and *for* you,
　　striving to present your call afresh to each new generation.
Work through them
　　that their words may bring people face to face
　　with the living Christ.
Speak your word of life,
　　your word of love.

We pray for Christians everywhere –
　　that their words and deeds may be a living witness,
　　testifying to your redeeming and renewing power.
Speak your word of life,
　　your word of love.

We pray for those new to faith,
　　those who, having responded, yearn to grow closer to you,
　　yet who may be unaware how best to do so.
Speak your word of life,
　　your word of love.

We pray for those whose faith is nominal,
　　those who consider themselves Christians
　　yet who have never seriously considered the gospel
　　or come to know you for themselves.
Speak your word of life,
　　your word of love.

We pray for those struggling in faith,
    those for whom the flame is spluttering,
    who find themselves wrestling
    with doubts, distractions or temptations
    that threaten to undermine their trust in you.
Speak your word of life,
    your word of love.

We pray finally for those who have lost their faith,
    their love grown cold,
    their enthusiasm faded,
    their trust destroyed.
Speak your word of life,
    your word of love.

Saving God,
    hear our prayer,
    and communicate afresh your gracious purpose
    and redeeming love,
    that our broken world may find healing and hope in you,
    through Jesus Christ our Lord.
Amen.

Closing prayer
Send us back, Lord,
    to our homes,
    our work,
    our friends
    and our families,
    resolved to love more deeply,
    serve more effectively
    and know you more fully,
    through Jesus Christ our Lord.
Amen.

**Order of
Service**

- Key verse
- Introduction
- Hymn
- Prayer of praise
- Reading
- Puzzles 1 and 2
- Prayer of thanksgiving
- Hymn
- Reading
- Puzzles 3 and 4
- Talk
- Prayer of confession
- Hymn
- Puzzle 5
- Prayer of intercession
- Hymn
- Closing prayer

APPENDIX

What do you see?

↑ Straight or curved lines?

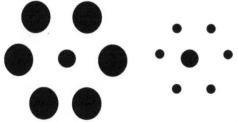

Which of the ↑
central circles
is the biggest?

↓ Duck or rabbit?

← The word Liar or a face?

↑ How many faces?

← How many circles are there in the grid?

↑ Faces or vases?

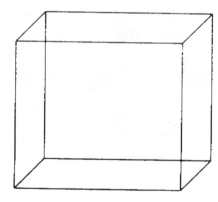

↑ Which is the front and which the back?

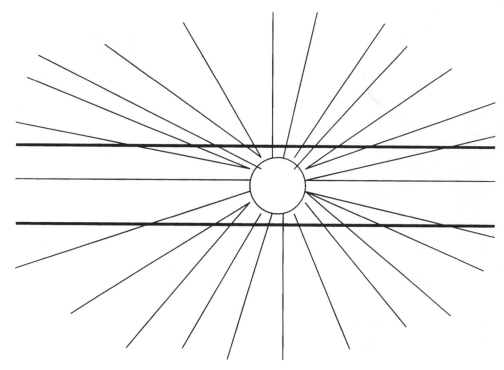

↑ Are the two bold horizontal lines curved or straight?

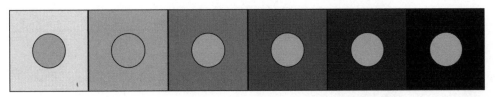

↑ Which of the central dots is the lightest?

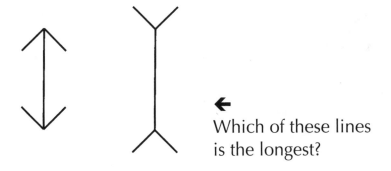

← Which of these lines is the longest?